DENNY MACK

GW00633911

BY
DENIS MCNAMARA

Personal Comment

I've always wanted to say this. All knowledge is second hand. The greatest intellectuals of our time or any other time must know that in comparison to the supreme being that put the whole universe together, with the millions of satellites, meteors, planets and stars swirling around in the limitless stratosphere, all in their own orbit, held in their orbits by a super magnetic power, is light years ahead of human comprehension. That same super power gave us relatively speaking a limited capacity to understand his super masterpiece. We are beginning to get smart when we realize how little we know in comparison to that Supreme Being, some of us call God.

FOREWORD

I am talking about a man who would take on any challenge, not just to prove a point, but his determination, to put his ability and succeed in whatever his goals were. His final ambitions were to get into some business that he knew instinctively he could succeed in. Let me tell you, the one he chose, happened to be a monumental challenge and that was, The Marble and Granite Industry. This industry is steeped with old time companies, that have controlled the industry for at least one hundred and fifty years, but, he reasoned that, with a bit of luck, a couple of good contacts, and a friend or two, and a lot of Moxie, it might see him through.

I can't give you the answer now, but it sure will be interesting to see how it all plays out. The answer of course will take a couple of years or much more, to find out if he is successful. I know he will be very confident, he can pull it off. In the meantime, keep your fingers crossed, and offer a little prayer for a kind hearted and great friend.

R.F.K.T

I am Denis McNamara, born March 10th 1925, and this is my story. There were eleven children in our family, seven girls and four boys. I will start with the oldest Vera. Vera raised most of us, in that I mean, she cooked, sewed and washed all of us, except my father, he washed occasionally. Today we would call his washing efforts, a bird bath and I'll tell you they were few and far between. My mother, she was meticulous. She bird bathed every day, may she RIP. I was like my mother in that regard. I too liked to clean up every day. My three sisters, Lily RIP, Vera RIP, and Philomena, worked all their lives in Royal Dublin Golf Club, Clontarf, Co Dublin. Vera was the chef, an excellent one. Phil, was the bar maid, also a very efficient one, and Lily was the Manageress, and also very good at running the club. I used to visit them quite often and played a bit of golf there also. My usual four ball was Jim Bourke, Secretary of the Golf Club, Justice Shannon, a very well known judge in the Dublin area, Lily my sister, and myself. We were all very competitive. It was dog eat dog sort of a game. We played for half a crown a head, two and sixpence in the old money. That time there was eight half crowns in a pound. In that group, I am the last man standing.

Phil got married to Syl Edwards a Dublin Man. He worked in Dunlops, and remained in Dunlops until his retirement. They were happily married, with three girls in family, Fiona, Jackie and Ann.

My oldest sister Vera also married, Brendan Doyle, a Dublin man. They had three children Sean, Paula and Declan.

Second eldest, Lily, married Tommy Walsh, Carrick, Ballinabracky Parish. Tommy was a quiet, decent man. They had no children.

Sister Breeda also emigrated to England. She had two children, Paul and Christine. Breeda suffered from asthma in her youth, but grew out of it later in life. Paul, giant of a man, six foot five, married Cora. Paul was what's known in England as a Chippie. He has a very nice business, a beautiful home and hospitality galore if you visit them.

Sister Ita is still hale and hearty. The youngest of the family, married Bill Heavey from Rhode. Bill passed away recently. They had four children, Frank, Pat, Marie and Catherine. Ita was a great table tennis player. Leinster champion at one stage of her career, learned the trade in Jim Haughtons old shop. She was as light of foot as a city beggar.

Mat, was one of the youngest of the family. He emigrated to England early in his life, and was fairly successful in the construction business.(no family). My two sisters Anna Mary and Agnes also emigrated. Agnes to England, and Anna Mary to U.S.A. Very sadly they both died young. Anna Mary (51yrs), Agnes (50yrs). They both passed away the same week. I was personally devastated. I got them hooked up on the phone, to say goodbye to each other. Sad, to this very day I get wasted thinking about that sad time in my life and also the lives of both their families, may the lord have mercy on both of them and all my fallen sisters, and also my brother, Murphy's Goats, Mick. Most every big family has a black sheep, Mick was ours. Mick loved a pint and wasn't too particular how he got the money to pay for the pint. One particular day he had a huge hangover, he always knew when he was hung over, that he would get a Haler. A Haler simply meant a few more pints to quench the thirst. So he stole my father's bike, and off he went in search of the field of goats. They belonged to a Mrs. Murphy, RIP from a towns land called the Strand. They were all milking goats. In his mind, mission accomplished. He knew the Moloneys travelling people were camped just a half mile away. He went there, spoke to Jim, the

Bossman and said to Jim, "I have a few goats for sale and better still they are milking goats". Jim said to him, "do you own them?" "Oh god of course I own them, I wouldn't be selling them if I didn't own them" Mick said. Jim came over and picked six of the best goats. "How much do you want for them", says Jim? "Ten pounds", Mick replied. Jim said," I'll give you one price take it or leave it, six pounds". Mick quickly replied, "It's a done-deal". How sweet it was for Mick, his thirst will soon be relieved.

Mrs. Murphy came down to the field, to bring home the goats, to milk them, as she did every evening. But to her amazement six of the best milking goats were gone. She's walking down the road scratching her head and she met this man on a bicycle. He said "you look like you're in a spot of trouble". "I am in trouble", she said, explaining to the man about her goats being missing from the field. "That's strange", he said. "There are a few goats down at the Travelers' camp, would they be your goats?" They must be. She went down and true enough they were her goats. She spoke to Jim, the Bossman, and told him, they were her goats. "Well", he said, "I bought them from Mick Mack; he said they were his goats". "That's enough about that", she said. "You should have known Jim". Jim was a true gentleman, he brought the six of them back to the field, and said, "Don't worry, I'll be visiting Mr. McNamara". Meanwhile Mick's mission was accomplished, the thirst quenched, he drank a rake of pints.

The next evening, who arrived at Mick's door, the one and only Jim Moloney. "Is Mick inside?" he asked my mother RIP. "He is", she said, "Is he in trouble again"? "Ah, not much – six pounds worth". Mick came out, with a big shit eating grin on him. "You owe me six pounds Mick". "Where would I get six pounds, I have four left, I'll give you that, and give me a couple of days to get the other two pounds", Mick said. Moloney ever the gentleman said "I'll give you the two days". Mick's brains were on Idol, but now they were back on overdrive again. He's scratching his head thinking, where will I get two pounds in two days. He got a sudden brain wave, as he often did before. He's looking across the old farm yard at a good flock of chickens. Wasn't that a bit of luck he said to himself. Jim Hamilton in the morning he mutters to himself. Met Jim the next morning down the road a good bit, a big bargaining session with Jim. He gave Mick thirty bob not a penny more. Mick was trying for the two pounds. He is still ten shillings and one day left short. He went to Moloney with the thirty shillings, and said to Moloney, "We have a big bank of turf, come and get the ten shillings worth". Again ever the gentleman Moloney accepted. They had Maloney's turf loaded on the trailer, and Mick said "take another ten shilling worth; I have a big thirst on me". Again Moloney agreed, and everybody got paid, and Mick was looking forward to the Village tonight for a few pints. It was just like in a smaller way today's bad debt, someone will lose out. In this episode it was my Mother. By the way, she asked Mick, what did he think happened the chickens? Mick thought she might ask that question and had already spread a few feathers and invited my mother, "look for yourself Mother", he said. And poor mother said, "The damned foxes". "How right you are mother", end of story. But not the end of Mick he will rise again.

I have three sisters still hanging in there, Phil, Breeda, Ita and two brother's Eamonn and Mat. Six at the time of writing this story are still alive.

Eamonn was the second youngest boy in the family, and the second smartest boy in the class, so said Master Carey. I wonder would he know, he always told my father that I was the smarter; let's say that is a matter of opinion. Eamonn worked as a shop boy in Fays', Edenderry for a few years, before he went to England. He joined the RAF there for a few years and I suppose he picked up a lot of knowledge in the RAF. Towards the end of his RAF years he met his wife Jackie. By the way, they were great together, over fifty years. She passed away recently, may she RIP. Eamonn was a bright man, forget what The Teacher said. He went to school at night for years, and eventually walked out of Southampton College with his Masters degree in Mathematics. No mean feat for a country farmer's son from Clonmore, Edenderry, Co.Offaly. He and his wife Jackie, both with their degrees taught for years in the college, where they themselves earned their degrees. Together they were a powerhouse of knowledge. But you would never know it, humility oozed from both of them. Lesson learned, dedication and determination will get you there, whatever your goals are, if you have the little gray matter up top. They had four in family, all girls. They all got married and went their own separate ways. I wish them well.

I remember my first day in school, just like it was yesterday. The teacher's name was Mrs. Bracken. I will never forget how kind she was, I knew right away I would like coming to school. She gave me two sweets, and said "Denis, suck them as they are hard and might break your teeth". I did exactly what she told me.

I spent the next three years in her classroom, and I must say I liked every moment of it. I though bad of leaving it and of course I hadn't the slightest idea what I was in for. When I moved to the other side of the Partition.

But I and all the other Pupils got a rude awakening. To say I was walking into a correctional facility wouldn't be greatly exaggerated. There was no hugging or greetings, just straight into the Combat Zone. The teacher's name was Mr. X, originally from Ballyhagen, Carbury, Co.Kildare. He very sincerely tried to teach all the pupils, admittedly he did go hard on some of them, unfortunately they weren't the smartest ones and he would use the enforcer a lot, (The Cane). He definitely wasn't the most popular person in the parish at that stage. In today's world you would not get away with that, you would have to answer to the Law of the Land.

Now, my own personal dealings with The Teacher. He would say to me out of the blue, Donnaca, gaelic for Denis. "You are staying at our house tonight, I was talking to your parents and they said it was alright for Denis to stay over". I knew he was not talking to my parents. There were no phones then, People in those days were so intimidated they were going to go along with The Teacher. I couldn't do anything about it. Luckily they were only one night-stands. Let me give you a sample, dinner over, we read some books, with The Teacher's family, all boys. I was sleeping with Mr X. Now everybody is paying attention. I will set the record straight, he never put a hand on me, God is my judge. But, after eating a hearty dinner, he (The Teacher) had steak and a large plate of onions and a pint of Guinness. He was over-ripe and his valves were registering one hundred plus, until they finally gave way, (save in your presence), he let go a whole string of farts, and simultaneously pulled the big cover over both our heads, so he thought? I had the cover tucked neatly around my neck. "Donnaca, quickly get that into your lungs, it will do you good, it's pungent", he said. The little whiff I got was the worst ever, and I haven't forgotten it. He was a legend in the Parish, but for mostly the wrong reasons. I think he finished his life in some kind of rehab. But he left an indelible mark on the young folk that attended Castlejordan National School. If you asked the older folk in his time, they would just shake their heads or dummy up.

This morning, there was very heavy rain. I can never come to terms with the decision of the parents of that era, to send their children to school in a downpour of rain. I'm talking about one mile or more. This particular incident I'm going to write about, was about a young boy, who went to school with four other of his family, and yes it rained that morning, very heavily. The distance they walked in those conditions was two miles. When I say they were wet, I mean soaking to the skin. In those days we weren't and they weren't privileged to have the proper water proofed overcoats, no they had like we all had, hand me downs from your older brothers and sisters, and instead of keeping out the rain, they actually attracted it. You can imagine how those poor kids felt, when that water started to reach their skin, and it did, and nothing they could do about it, stay there all day long freezing their poor little butts off, while the steam was visible. The teacher was standing with his big fat arse, in front of the fire, just in case a little heat might get out to the children, all of a sudden, he got a brain wave, and said, "Hey, BogTrotter, come up here", it seems he was correcting the papers from yesterday, and maybe this kids wasn't too good. But the kid didn't answer, to BogTrotter, and he, the teacher said it again. The teacher has a very bad temper, and actually shouted the boy's name, and he came up to him and as he was on his way up the teacher met him, caught him by his side burns and dragged him a bit, and let go, and as he let him go, he drew out with his other hand, and hit his opposite jaw. Then went for what he called "the persuader", a hefty cane. He muttered something like, "you'll learn the next time, and you'll also be in time for school". You see, the boy was about five minutes late, and he was also taking that out on him. He hit him, the poor kid, six times on each hand. His two hands were actually blue, a heartless brute of a man. The boy did not respond to it this time either.

I want you the reader to think about that, and imagine it was your boy. You probably would feel the way, I did that morning, if I was big enough, and had a weapon in my hand, I think I was angry enough to do him a lot of bodily damage. But that was wishful thinking. I have a feeling that, that boy did not complain to his parents, and if he did, they never did anything about it. I complained once, to my parents, I knew they would do nothing about it. In fact they agreed unanimously that I didn't get half enough of a beating. The parents of that era were totally intimidated, they were afraid to challenge authority.

It was actually a throwback to the penal times, the philosophy was, a shut mouth catches no flies. That fear was instilled in our parent's minds, and you all know by whom. Thank God we have our independence, and that peace has broken out at last, and time has been a great healer.

The following will to a great extent be my own story. With my wife Mona always included where appropriate. That is an understanding between us No Doubt.

About the age of twenty I started to get very interested in football (Gaelic) and coincidentally at around that time 1945, give or take a year, the Reverend Callary, was moved or appointed to the parish of Castlejordan & Ballinabrackey. What a coincidence. He too loved the game and as I found afterwards, quite a brilliant coach.

He (Fr.Callary, of course), got together about twenty five of the best in the parish. He really had to go deep age-wise to get that many. We had a good field – Boyne Park. He laid down the rules to us, and basically what he meant, was, if at any time you don't like the heat, leave the kitchen.

We lined up twice a week in the evening of course, and slowly, but surely he started to find a place for us in the team. Finally he decided on fifteen of us and our places as well. Now I'm not going to tell you who we played.

By the way in the Junior Championship, I will tell you we played nine times, we won five of them and lost four. You will have to agree with me it was a great achievement for Father

Callary and he actually was delighted. I played where I always liked to play (center field), I and Fr.Callary was happy with that. His philosophy was to stay with some of the guys until they either proved him right or wrong. He had a selection committee and had no problem listening to their advice but he wouldn't act on the spur of the moment, he gave everybody a fair shake and that was an admirable trait in the man. After having a few losing seasons, a few prospects started to appear, like Ned Carey (John Conlon,Rev), Jimmy Coyne, we started to get ideas that we might go places, and Fr.Callary arranged a game with his own alma mater, St.Finnians College, Mullingar. He got his press core together and advertised on every rag paper in sight. Whatever he did, it worked, a great crowd showed up at Boyne Park, the press core from all the county papers, and the local ones showed up as well.

This wasn't just any game. This was a showdown between the best college team around, and the up and coming Ballinbrackey junior team. Fr.Callary gathered the Bracks around him, he said "listen carefully, this college team is made up of all young boys between sixteen and eighteen years of age, you are all grown up mature men. I don't want you to do anything mean or dirty. In other words take it easy on them at all costs. God bless now and good luck". The throw in and Neddie Mitchell wasn't refereeing. The Bracks didn't think they needed him as it turned out the Bracks would have needed a couple of Neddie Mitchells, but as umpires, to disallow all the goals, Finians scored. You remember I said earlier in this story that we were beginning to get ideas. Fr.Callary was no fool. He knew how good Finians were, and this would bring us down to earth. It did, two years later we were in the Junior County Final. Fr.Callary got a double dose of satisfaction, his old team winning big and teaching us the lesson of a life time. P.S we were beaten in the Junior Final, but we enjoyed the wins leading up to it. Now I was getting to be about twenty three years old. I got a letter from the county board, that I was selected to play in the Meath Junior team. Longford in Mullingar. It was very handy, I drove to it myself. We beat Longford by a few points. I was in England with an uncle for a few weeks and when I came back Meath were playing Wicklow in the Leinster Final, and I played in that game at Croke Park. Wicklow beat us, and we were out of the Junior scene for that year.

In 1948, Meath seniors were playing Cavan in Breffini Park, and I was picked on that team. The wettest day you could imagine. I played on John Joe O'Reilly. That was some baptism, between him and the downpour I was so happy to hear the final whistle. Final score, Cavan eighteen points, Meath three. Frankie Byrne said in the locker room after the game, "This team with a few switchers can beat that Cavan team". There wasn't one guy in the locker room, that didn't think he was nuts. He explained this way, Paddy O'Brien who played centre field, will be our new full back. Paddy Dixon will be our centre back, and we will build the team around them. Now I ask anybody who knows Gaelic football, was that prophetic or what? Frankie Byrne deserves to be put on a pedestal with the likes of Colmcille, no I am not kidding.
Step up to the plate for your award Frankie; I know you are hail and hearty Frankie, because my sister Phil Edwards talks to you at church in Clontarf all the time.

Now Meath met Cavan in the All Ireland 1949 Final – and as all Gaels know Meath beat them just like Frankie Byrne predicted. That Cavan team was considered one of the best ever. 1950 League Final, played in April '51, Meath v Mayo. I was on the panel for that game. I was a sub, didn't get any playing time, but I wasn't complaining. There was a trip to New York coming up, and believe or not, it was for a whole month. Isn't that incredible, we had the time of our lives. The American people were so generous; of course they were either Irish from Ireland or Irish Americans. I will never forget their generosity. The whole trip was super, and of course what made it even more memorable, the Galway hurlers were with us, no scarcity of a drop of poi teen.

I met people of all nationalities, it was a great experience, and to get a perspective on the different customs and habits of other nationalities. Somebody once said, you can't beat the travelled man. I think it was my friend Father Dan Moore.

We played New York in the League Final in Gaelic Park, in the Bronx, New York. Up to that time it was the First League final ever played outside Ireland, and I am not sure if it is the only one ever played outside the country.

John O'Donnell worked hard to get that concession, as he was the owner of Gaelic Park. It was a great achievement for him. However, he was just as unhappy when Meath beat his New York team. New York, some fine footballers, guys like Big Pat McAndrews, and Bill Carlos. Meath just beat them with a brilliant goal by Mattie McDonald, Ballinlough. Mattie was my roommate in the Hotel in Manhattan, New York, Room 1014, and The Henry Hudson Hotel. In that game I played about ten minutes. While I was in New York I met a man from Offaly, and he said to me, "If you ever come back to New York, or think about coming over, get in touch with me", and gave me his address and phone number. "You will have your place on the Offaly Football team". That Offaly have always a strong football team, Meath have just a very poor Junior team, due to the fact that there was hardly any emigration from Meath. I thanked him and told him if ever I decided to go to the states, I would be in touch. Poetic words, but one never knows what's around the corner, and at that time I didn't think I would be going anywhere except the old farm in Clonmore.

Looking back over the years, the most outstanding thing that sticks out in my mind was my football career, if you could call it that, and Paddy Dixon, picking me up at the old homestead in Clonmore. That particular time, Meath played very often. From 1949 to 1955, Meath played one hundred and one games, between league and championship, Byrne Cup, Played Mayo in London's Wembley Stadium, four Easters in a row, and a few other Cup games. It came to one hundred and one. They tallied up ninety eight wins, two draws and one loss. That will take a lot of beating. At that period in time, Meath were almost unbeatable. I was on the panel, all that time, and I told you the reason why, earlier in the story. I won't go down that road again. Meath broke several records in the series of wins that many never be equaled. Very few people actually are aware of that. I don't know if many people outside of Meath would be too interested. I just thought I would mention it. The most enjoyable time, which lasted one month – can you believe, one month, with the Meath Football Team in the U.S. Mostly New York, the other city was Boston for a couple of days. I played about ten or twelve minutes in the polo grounds, in the league final which we won. Thanks to Matty McDonald with that marvelous goal.

For a brilliant goal with two minutes to go, we were down by a point, but that goal pretty much sowed it up for us. They didn't score, afterwards, a very good New York team, Paddy Dixon accidentally ran into Big Pat McAndrew, and Pat had to be carried off. Big Pat was controlling the centre of the field at the time. John O'Donnell, was fuming when Matty McDonnell scored that all important goal. John said, McDonnell pushed Bill Carlos, just enough for Matty to catch the ball and race towards the goal and shook the back of the net for that winning goal. J.O'Donnell really gave the referee a real hard time about that free. But full time came and Meath were victorious, and tomorrow we are going on a cruise around Manhattan, to celebrate. There will be dinner and the medals will be presented on board. A joyous occasion. Thursday, we are headed to Boston, and will be there for the weekend. We won that game. Paddy O'Brien hurt his finger training and he could not tog out, so Paddy suggested to Fr.Tully, that he thought, judging from training practice, the best high catcher, after himself, would be Dinney McNamara, and so I got the job. I caught some nice high balls. I also kicked out some pretty long balls. I was delighted with that, and at the dinner that night, they presented us with nice medals. This by the way is Sunday night, and we will be on our way back tomorrow evening to New York, but we will get in some more sight-seeing around the lovely city of Boston.

Travelling to the States in those days was a great bonus. The fact that it was a League Final was the reason we were there, and as I said before I stand corrected, but that was the only League Final up to that time. So that, for me personally was a great game to win, it was a very special honor, and I'm happy to have that League Medal. New York was in the final for their first time too. We marched up Fifth Avenue, and were met on the steps of City Hall, by the then Mayor, Bill O'Dwyer. We were togged out in our football gear. I remember it was a little chilly that day, so we couldn't wait to get back into our clothes. A nice meal in a nearby restaurant, a few speeches. Bill O'Dwyer, the Mayor was a Mayo man, so he spoke about the friendly rivalry between Mayo and Meath that still exists to this day. We also got a great reception, when we landed back in our native shore, in good old Dublin City, and a welcoming hand shake from the personable, Alfie Byrne, The Lord Mayor of Dublin. After refreshments, and meeting all our friends, we said our goodbyes, to one another; we were on our way home and not looking forward to getting back to the old drudgery again, not the greatest scenario to be looking forward to. We will stay in a good frame of mind, and with great memories of our wonderful trip and the hospitality we received in New York City.

However, I never really got any commitment from my father about the farm, or if indeed if I would ever get it. I kept playing a bit of football with the Bracks, that B.B team were very good. Man for man we had the best B.B team, ever, but we just didn't come through on the big occasions. We were beaten in several finals, including the foggy Sunday, visibility; I kid you not, eight yards. It was measured with a fog-meter, Gospel truth. The highlight of that game was Brian Carroll missing a goal from four yards. He must have known if he got that goal it would be disallowed, as he was in the square, and so as there would be no confusion, he did the right thing, he kicked it wide. You would have to agree, he was smart. There were better days ahead. At that particular time, I was subbing on the Meath team. Nearly always first sub, and I often wondered, why I wasn't getting more playing time. I never mentioned my suspicions to anybody at that time, but one day, I was playing golf with Paddy O'Brien, and he said, "I was always trying to get you on the team and after seeing you in the training camp, I was even more determined to get you on". It had fallen on deaf ears, so he told me he would take it a step further. He was very good friends with Jack Fitzgerald. At that time, Jack Fitzgerald was chairman of the Leinster Council, and on the Meath selection committee. Jack got in touch with his buddy, Ted Meade. Ted wrote him back and said, "I am well aware of the Denis McNamara problem". I didn't know I was causing a problem, I was actually embarrassed. Ted went on and told Jack Fitz, the reason he is not getting on and never will while I have anything to do with the selection committee, is that 'We' the county board get a letter almost every Tuesday or Wednesday, that Denis McNamara had been playing Rugby with Edenderry at the weekend. The name. The letter writer was none other than Mr. X. Before I heard all this Mr.X was deceased, and I had finished playing football. We probably would have had a few words at least.

Thanks to Paddy O'Brien, it did satisfy my suspicions. I will always be grateful Paddy, that's what friends are for, (good friends).

I am getting to be in my thirties, and time to get my life organized for the future. I am going to sit down with the bank manager and my father and see if I am getting the farm, or will it be emigration. We met one night in the bank. The booze was good for a while, but then the good humor changed. The manager and then myself, we made our cases, but to no avail. My father said, "You fellows are pissing up stream and against the wind as well", end of story. Meeting ended, and I am bound for America. I wasn't really disappointed, as I couldn't see myself doing that kind of work for a living. I really always thought it was a tough way to make a living. I was going out with a girl from Ballyboggan, Mona Coyne. We discussed what happened, she was delighted and said "We're off to the States".

I left Ireland, I must say rather sadly, when the time came. I sailed to the United States July 22nd, 1957. I had everything arranged with my two friends, Paddy Grimes, who sponsored me. That was a big deal then and Paddy Egan, a great Offaly Gael. He originally came from Birr. I went down to Cobh in County Cork, the evening before with my beautiful girlfriend, Mona Coyne, Ballyboggan, and our great and true friends, Mick Moriarity the one and only, a great Kerry man and Ollie Powell my first cousin. Gene Coyne was also with us in Cobh. We had a memorable night together but sad I went out on the tender the next morning. I must say Mona and I were really heartbroken and as the New Amsterdam sailed away into the mist, I can say I was as low as you could get. I just prayed that Mona and my friends would get back home safe. It took ten days to cross the Atlantic Ocean, and we landed in New York on the 22nd of August 1957, and there to eet us were my good old friends. Jimmy Corcoran, Paddy Egan and also Pete McDermot, another great Gael, all Offaly men. Paddy Egan was driving and I didn't know exactly where I would be staying, but Paddy told me, I was staying with him until they got me fixed up in digs, not to worry. We had a great chat on the way back to Paddy's home. These three guys were men of the world, and they said as soon as we got to Paddy's, you'll be a little tired and maybe a bit lonely, so you're going to lie down for an hour or two, and it will do you the world of good, which I did, and I felt nice and refreshed, and chatted some more. It was now about six in the evening. Pete and Jim were going home. "You and I Denis, will go for a bite to eat in this place called The Riverdale Diner", said Paddy, which was just around the corner on "Broadway". It was and still is the best known diner in the north east Bronx. It was a favorite haunt for all the Irish in that neck of the woods. Gaelic Park was a quarter of a mile up the street from it. It was popular with the teams when they came out to play in Gaelic Park. After a nice meal Paddy and I went back to his place. We watched television for a couple of hours and retired early.

The next morning, we were up bright and early, it was Saturday. Riverdale Diner again, lovely breakfast, bacon, eggs, sausages and coffee. How about that for great treatment. Now Paddy said "we'll do a bit of a tour, I will show you the Bronx, or some of it anyway". Fordham Road and the famous Fordham University, what a beautiful shopping centre all Irish at one point in history, but you could see it was beginning to change, what a pity. He drove by a very famous baseball stadium; you guessed it, Yankee Stadium, where some of the greatest players of all time played, for the Yankee's and other great players, from all the other teams across the USA. I knew names like Di Maggio, Mantle, Moose Showron, Yogi Berra and many more played in Yankee Stadium for years.

After a lot of driving, where did we wind up, your right again, Riverdale Diner. "Dinner time", I said to Paddy, "I am not like this, I want to buy you dinner". Paddy replied "No way Denis, I have money from the club to take care of you". "Well you tell the club, I really appreciate this hospitality". "Denis you are going to be playing in a few tough games, you can strut your stuff, one week from tomorrow, and we are playing Leitrim in the Semi-Final of the New York Championship. You will be centre half back. Johnny Roger, former Louth Player will be on your right and Jim McGeoghan, Longford country player will be on your left". "Sounds good to me", I said.

After a week enjoying the hospitality of Paddy Egan, I am now in new digs. A lovely woman and why wouldn't she, she was from Tullamore. We got along great. She looked after me like I was her own son. The game is on tomorrow against Leitrim, so I got a good night's sleep and I can't let the team down after all this royal treatment. Started at 3.30pm, was over at 5pm. We won but not without a good tussle. I believe we beat them five points. I could tell by the reception I got, I must have done alright. The paper came out Wednesday, and the Irish Echo headline said "Casey the More Polished but McNamara the Power House of the Game". Myself and Paddy Casey really celebrated that victory. But there were stiffer opposition on the horizon. In two weeks time, the name of the opposition was Cork. Loaded with ex county players, and that included a couple of friends of mine, Johnny Creedon and Denis Bernard, I was at the same table with them on the ship on our way out to the states. It is now Big Game Day, Gaelic Park full to capacity. This Cork team beat the Louth all Ireland champions just a couple of months ago and are favorites to win this New York Championship Final.

Reception at City Hall, New York: *The acting Mayor of New York, Mr T Sharkey, greeting Mr Michael Keogh, President of the Gaelic Athletic Association. Included are: Rev. Fr. P Tully (Meath) and Rev. Fr. M Walsh (Galway)*

MEATH PEN PICTURES FROM 1951

Name	Club	Age	Height ft. ins.	Weight lbs.	Occupation:
Kevin Smith	Naas	29	6'0"	182	Shop Assistant
Mick O'Brien	Skryne	27	5'10"	161	Clerk
Paddy OBrien	Sean McDermotts	26	6'1"	196	Insurance Salesman
Kevin McConnell	Syddan	27	5'11"	172	Farmer
Seamus Heery	Rathkenny	24	5'9"	182	Farmer
Connie Kelly	Oldcastle	25	5'9"	168	Farmer
Christo Hand	Sean McDermotts	26	5'8"	168	Lorry Driver
Paddy Connell	Sean McDermotts	24	6'0"	168	Fruit Wholesaler
Des Taaffe	St. Dympna's	24	6'1"	196	Mental Nurse
Frank Byrne	O'Mahonys	27	5'8"	161	Teacher
Mattie McDonnell	Ballinlough	21	5'11"	182	Farmer
Paddy Meegan	Syddan	29	5'8"	168	Farmer
Brian Smyth	Skryne	27	5'10½"	168	Bus Driver
Jimmie Reilly	Dunboyne	25	5'9½"	182	Building Contractor
Peter McDermott	O'Mahonys	32	5'10"	182	Egg/poultry wholesaler
Pat Carolan	Kilmainhamwood	24	5'9½"	168	Cattle Dealer
Denny McNamara	Ballinabrackey	24	5'10"	175	Farmer
Paddy Dixon	Ballivor	27	5'11"	196	Haulage Contractor
Bob Rusk	Dunboyne	22	5'10"	168	Salesman
Lar McGuinness	Nobber	27	5'11"	175	Farmer

The Meath panel which lost to Mayo in the 1951 All-Ireland final (from left) was: Back - L. McGuinness, J. Reilly, P. Connell, D. Taaffe, A. Foran, M. McDonnell, K. Smyth, B. Smyth, P. Dixon, D. McNamara; front - P. Carolan, M. O'Brien, F. Byrne, K. McConnell P. O'Brien, S. Heery, P. Meegan, P. McDermott, C. Kelly, C. Hand, R. Ruske.

READY TO TAKE OFF – The Meath team and officials at Shannon Airport prior to their flight to America.

ARRIVAL IN NEW YORK - The Meath and Galway teams with officials photographed on arrival at New York

The throw in and the game is on. Cork gets the first point and you could tell from the applause that Cork had a large crowd of supporters, but Offaly came right back with a point of their own, level pegging after five minutes, you could sense that this was not going to be a runaway victory for either sides. The next ten minutes, they scored a point apiece, fifteen minutes gone, two points each. The marking is tough and close. The crowds are in tender hooks. They score four points each before half-time, with the score reading with five minutes to half time Cork adds two point, four points for Offaly, six points for Cork. They get a very much needed break; the temperature was ninety-five degrees. Sweat pumping out of us. The throw in after half-time, Offaly break away with a long well placed drop kick by D McNamara, plucked out of the air by Paddy Casey to Ivor Quigley who ran for about ten yards and shook the back of the net. Needless to say the Offaly supporters went berserk, and why not, that score created a momentum that landed another great point by Mickey Furlong, no better man to rally a team. Cork looked to be in bad trouble. Never count Cork out. When down they rallied and had two great points, they were back in the game big time! After ten minutes of no scoring, the marking was ferocious, Cork broke through, Denis Bernard got it I think he had goal in mind. He hit it very hard and it just got over the bar. It's a one point game, Offaly defense is holding, McNamara showing a lot of experience, clearing several dangerous balls, one in particular was caught by Paddy Casey, raced in again and drove it over the bar. Now it's a two point game with about three minutes left. Cork attack, two minutes left, the ball is virtually on the Offaly goal line, and out of the blue scoops McNamara, several Cork guys hit him trying to get him and the ball over the line, but he cleared it about forty yards down the line, Offaly not out of danger. Johnny Creedon took the sideline kick. He told me after he meant to drop it a little short, and somebody might get lucky and connect for a goal, but he hit that little bit too hard and it drifted wide, Cork had their chances, but you would have to say Offaly were just that little bit better. The kick out and full time is up.

Final Score / Offaly 1-8 Cork 1-6. (I am writing this taken from a taped commentary of the game).

The Offaly Team,
who won the New York Championship in 1967

The following information some people might like to know. The one's of us who like Gaelic Hurling and Football. How did "Jones Road" get its name Croke Park, one of the best known addresses in the country. You might ask who was "Jones" and why would a road be called after him? He was born in County Meath in 1759. Frederick Edward Jones began life, with all the privileges of wealth and position. He was educated at Trinity College, Dublin, and spent some years on the continent, doing the grand tour as was the custom for people of his rank. Jones was six feet tall and considered very handsome, and to be a pleasant companion, an honorable gentleman, he was given the nickname "Buck".

After his return from the continent Jones and Lord Westmeath purchased a music hall in Fishamble Street in Dublin and set up a theatre. It opened March 6th, 1793 with the "Beggars Opera" and "The Irish" performed by distinguished amateurs. In 1794 he was given permission to open a theatre for seven years in Dublin, but not to take money at the door. He leased the dilapidated Crow street theatre and spent a fortune refurbishing it until it was considered one of the finest houses in Dublin. It opened in 1796, but was closed a few weeks later when martial law was imposed.

His luck did not improve. In 1807 Richard Brinsley Sheridan invited Jones to purchase a share in the famed Drury Lane Theatre, but it burned down two years later. Back in Dublin Crow Street Theatre was wrecked in riots in 1814 and 1819.

Buck Jones private life was centered on his house in North Dublin. He bought the house and the lands, known as Patrick's Grove and decided to restore the original name "Clonliffe House". In his time the lands extended as far back as the River Tolka, and included a piece of land known as Donnelly's Orchard. Clonliffe Road in those days was a narrow winding lane, and the only access to it was from Drumcondra Road at one end and Ballybough at the other. So to provide access to his house, Jones had a new road made. It was a continuation of Russell Street, and went over a temporary bridge across the Royal Canal opposite his house.

For many years this was known as Buck Jones Road, but as time went on it was shortened to Jones's Road. I personally liked Buck Jones's Road better.

His bad luck with the theatre business continued. His permit was not renewed by the government because of his political views, and he was convinced, they didn't like him. In 1820, the once wealthy "Buck Jones" was imprisoned for bad debt, (Where was NAMA then? I am sure they would have taken him on), but Buck's three sons remained and continued in the theatre. On his release from prison he lived in a small cabin near where Mount Joy Square stands today. He died in 1834, but his name will always live on with the iconic Croke Park located on the famous address. No doubt Buck Jones left us memories that we are all very proud of, in today's world, somebody would have made a movie about the life and times of Buck Jones, the swashbuckling character, that was well known by rich and poor. Of course today Croke Park is one of the great sports stadiums of the world. Nowhere on the planet will you see a more spacious and beautiful pitch, its size is not equaled anywhere. I personally played on it, it's a revelation, and you feel like a spring in your step. I would argue that its one of, if not the best playing surface in the world, and it should be with about five foot deep of cinders to keep it as near perfect as possible, and with all the facilities in the interior, food, beverages and all kinds of goodies. If Buck Jones could only see it now, he would certainly be amazed. It's a great monument to all those who made this dream a reality. It gives so much pleasure to so many, and will for years to come.

Some interesting history about Unions in New York. There was an Irish Man in the 1950's hitting the headlines in New York area. He became very well known in the labour movement, and was a huge and sometimes a controversial figure in the United States as founder and first President of the powerful Transport Workers Union. Not too many people have a bus depot in Manhattan named after them, but he did, as well as accomplishing a good many other achievements. He is certainly not forgotten in Kilgarvan either, with a visitor's centre in the converted St Peter's Church. Mike Quill landed in New York on St Patrick's Day 1926. He got a job with the I.R.T (Interborough Rapid Transport). This is the largest subway operator in the USA; about half of the transit company's workers were Irish. Michael Quill founded, The Transport Workers Union of America in 1934, and was elected as its first President, a position he held until his death in 1966.

It began with around 400 members but by 1937 and following affiliation with other unions, its members increased to 40,000 and more importantly became the official bargaining agent for all workers on New York's transit systems. Quill became a hero; his friendship became cemented down the years with the mayors of New York City. He certainly was a big factor in his support for Robert Wagner, when he became Mayor of New York City. But it wasn't the same with Mayor Lindsey, he challenged Quill in trying to negotiate an agreement, it broke down, and New York City was faced with its first strike. The strike was called and implemented on the basis of a wage dispute. The strike lasted ten days; eight million commuters were practically at a standstill. An injunction outlawing the strike was issued on the 1st of June 1966 promptly torn up by Quill. The Judge outlined an arrest order on the union leaders for violation of the injunction. The next morning at a press conference in the Americano Hotel Quill issued his noted words: "The judge can drop dead in his black robes". Taken to jail he was clearly not a well man. By this time he had to be rushed to Bellvue hospital for emergency treatment. From there he was transferred to Mount Sinai Hospital and finally allowed home. Three weeks after being jailed, the authorities capitulated and the union victory represented a huge improvement in the conditions of its workers. The package was worth sixty million dollars comprising a wage increase of about a dollar an hour, and extra paid holidays, increased pension benefits and other benefits as well. Quill gave his last press conference in the Americana Hotel in celebration a couple of weeks after the strike was over. He died at home, many people believed as a result of the excitement and stress of the hard campaign, at a time when he was not feeling well. The funeral mass took place in St Patrick's Cathedral, with tributes and testimonials from far and wide. One of his men, a conductor on the trains said "Without Mike Quill we would be working for pittance". From Martin Luther King, leading American Civil Rights activist, "Mike Quill was a fighter for decent things all his life including Irish Independence, and fair wages for labour. This is a man the ages will remember". I personally say he was both a good Irishman and a great Kerryman. Mike Quill was laid to rest at the Gate of Heaven Cemetery in Hawthorne, New York, as was my own sister Anna Mary. May they rest in peace

In the meantime Jim Corcoran brought me down to the Marble Union and introduced me to a business agent, and he told me to come and sit every day for a couple of hours and shortly there would be a job for me

I am looking forward to Mona coming, in case you forgot, my girlfriend, landing 26th October 1957. I'll be here just three months when she lands, I can't wait. I have secured a nice room for her, with a good Irish woman, Mrs. Hackett, and it's only a couple of blocks from where I am staying now, (at that time). Unfortunately, Mona had contacted some kind of flu on the way over on the plane. She was very sick, so I had to do everything I knew how, to get her well again. Mrs. Hackett was a big help. Plenty of juices and all kinds of medication. It took Mona a couple of weeks to get well again. She was very young, not twenty years yet. Plus she was very lonely and missed her mother and home.

Two weeks later, now she is almost back to normal. She wants to go to work, but I told her to take it easy for another week, and you'll be fully recovered. Two weeks later she got a job in Macy's department store. She didn't know the money very well, but there was a lovely person working right beside her, and never let her put a foot wrong, a real nice caring lady. While I was waiting to get into the Marble business, I also took a job in Macys. As we only lived one block from each other, we went to work together. One morning Mona got a terrible pain in her tummy. Luckily the train pulled into a station. The bathroom was right there. I think God arranged that, but lo and behold we needed a nickel to open the doors. This nice man realized the predicament we were in and handed us a nickel. Mona ran for it, and luckily just in time. What sweet relief. She said "I'll never forget the gripping pain in my tummy, may God bless the man with the nickel. I'll say a prayer for him". We celebrated the joy of getting over that crisis in a little coffee shop beside Macys, and Mona continued on there.

I got a job as an assistant, helper to a man who was installing the marble. It came in slabs; they were about four foot tall by seven foot wide. I would help him lift them. He showed me everything, how to mix the Plaster of Paris, I point the joints, etc., etc. It was so methodical, it was really a lot of common sense, and if you were interested it was easy picking it up. One of the best jobs I had while I was working for other marble contractors. I later got into business myself, in the World Trade Centre six years I spent there, most of it as the shop steward for the Marble Union and of course everybody on the planet knows what happened to the Trade Centre. All I'll say is May the good Lord take care of all their souls.

Getting back to Mona and me, it's now 1959 and we are planning to get married. I got an apartment on Sedgwick Avenue in the Bronx. We have set the date; it will be June 27th 1959. We are almost two years now in the States. We have all the arrangements made. Only one from either of our families came and that was Mona's uncle from Canada. Paddy Coyne, a giant of a man, (gentle giant). He gave Mona away and of course was a Six Footer, plus they looked absolutely stunning walking down the aisle in Saint Patricks Cathedral, 51st on Fifth Avenue, you might ask where were the relatives, but let me say, nobody was travelling overseas in those days, nobody, for the very simple reason, people couldn't afford it. That was then but, later on we had a nice lot of guests at the reception that was held in the Henry Hudson Hotel in 51st Manhattan. Mona's uncle Paddy, who gave her away, made a lovely speech as he said on behalf of all Coyne's that weren't there. I must say he spoke elegantly and we all danced into the late evening. It really was a great milestone in my life. I enjoyed the day very much, as did Mona. We were conscious of the fact that we didn't have family at the wedding, but we were very happy as we were going to Florida on our honeymoon.

My Wedding Day 27ᵗʰ June 1959

The hotel we were staying in was arranged by the man that married us, Fr. Mat Grehan from Ballinabrackey. No better man, a lovely man. He really looked after us. He joined us one day at the swimming pool and I'm glad he did. It was the kind of pool where they probably all are built, where it was ramped down towards the deep end which is usually 6'6" which was out of my depth. I got on the down slope of the pool and I couldn't stop, I didn't want to start shouting, I was embarrassed but more importantly I was close to drowning. Fr Mat copped it on right away and he was by my side in a flash, I was struggling so much, panicking, I nearly drowned him as well but he managed and towed me to shore. Needless to say I forever stayed far from deep ends of pools! He took us to some exotic night spots, lady bar maids, nothing on them bigger than a smile, but he never looked at one to tell the truth of him. "Priests don't". We had a memorable honey moon but for slightly the wrong reasons, we got badly sunburnt. We got burnt to the point we got sick to our stomachs, terrible feeling, no experience of tropical heat, up to that point in our lives. We spent a great last night with Mat (Rev.). He took us to a Private House, and the rest you will get it hard to believe.

We first went into this huge room as best as we could see Mona, me and Fr.Mat. Slowly a figure started appearing. First the head looked like a lion's head. Then the light, multi coloured of a real head , a real man sitting about twenty feet up on this podium on a huge decorative chair and the most elaborate looking piano you ever saw and he said "How are you Father Mat", it wasn't Fr. Mat's first visit here it seemed. "Oh I'm great" says Mat, "How are you Mario". "Great" he replied. "where are my servants?", like a flash a curtain flew back and there right in front of us was about ten servants, with little tables with wheels, they were wheeled in right up to us loaded with every kind of food and drink you could imagine, and right on top in a good hand book, was his repertoire of music for this evening. Some of the great semi- classics of the past twenty years, we knew almost all of them and so would you. He has a brilliant piano and he loved playing it, p.s, he was a huge man, that seat he sat on was an elevator, it came from the basement and he was sitting on it, but it was made to look like a chair. Fr. Mat told us he didn't mind anybody knowing how heavy he was, and that was five hundred and eighty pounds. He adored and loved playing music for his friends and he was reputed to be worth about twenty billion. "Before you go Father Mat" He said, "I would like to know the names of my guests", Fr. Mat gave him out names. "Denis and Mona McNamara, "well they will be entered on my visitor's roster". We said our goodbyes and thanked him. It was the most palatial home I've ever seen. Fr. Mat was telling us he did the same thing every week, he loves playing the piano and entertain his friends. Fr Mat also told us he says private mass there at least a couple of times a month and invites his close friends to participate and always entertains them. Did Mona and I ever dream we would be involved in such a unique and beautiful experience, on our honeymoon? We also felt very privileged to be good friends with Mat, from way back in Ireland , who made all this possible, St Patricks Cathedral, the beautiful hotel in Florida, the best restaurants in Florida, the whole bit. Needless to say we will always look back on it all as one of the happiest times of our lives.

Next week I'm sure will be a little different as its back to work. Mona has studied for her State Board Exam in a couple of weeks as she needs to be eligible to work here in the States. Work is plentiful in the marble business about two years on I'm thinking about quitting football. I will be playing this coming Sunday, maybe my last game. Sunday came and the game was on and as bad luck would have it I went up for a kick out and about three other lads, whatever way we got tangled up I'm on the ground. Yes you guessed it, a broken leg right at the knee. They brought me to the hospital in Yonkers which was close by. A famous bone surgeon then Dr. Daly met me at the emergency unit, "oh, Gaelic Park" he said in a loud voice, "get a couple of them every week from there". Then he said "don't be disheartened Denis, we will do the right thing for you. Very thoughtful of him he said "have you next of kin or a wife that you would like to call" I said "thanks very much I'd like to call my wife but at this very minute would you please give me a Pain Killer". "What do you think this is in my hand" he gave me the pain killer and told me to wait a minute, the pain will be gone and then you can call your wife. What a nice guy. I called Mona, luckily, she was there. This is now about five o'clock in the evening. "Hello love, I have a lovely dinner on for the two of us, don't be long now" she said. I said, to be truthful, I was a bit emotional, "I won't be home for dinner", she asked why and I replied I'm in the hospital in Yonkers, St Joseph's. She didn't speak for about a minute then she said "You broke your leg or something". Well I said "Not that bad, I fractured it". She said "I'll be up there shortly" and I said "Don't forget to turn off the stove". You would get it hard to believe the trauma this caused in our lives, at least for the time being, Dr. Daly had a full plaster cast on my leg by the time Mona arrived. She did the sensible thing she had the dinner before she left. (Big hand for Mona). When she got there we were both a little emotional but that passed like every other trauma, in life you have to learn how to handle the Bad and the Good.

The two weeks in Saint Joseph's hospital passed quickly and it was great to be home, during those six months with a full length cast, I've learnt the art of cooking. It was straight up, plain food, nothing fancy and at least Mona got a break, that six months passed pretty quickly, plenty of visitors, a couple of beers here and there helped pass the time with friends and now I'm into Re-Hab. There wasn't a muscle in that leg. I did the appropriate exercises every day for a number of hours and by the end of three months I was ready to go back to work. I went back to work coming up to 1960, worked mostly with the same company for all that time. 1961, our one and only daughter was born, Caroline, that caused the usual excitement with celebrations with friends and rituals and what seemed like no time, actually three years, our son Roger was born. He came into the world screaming and he's still at it some forty years later. I'm delighted to report they are doing well for themselves, Caroline, with two boys, Evan twenty years and Karl seventeen years old. The girl is the oldest, Lauren, and she is twenty four years old, doing Pharmacy, almost finished. Evan is a rugby player. He's quite good at it, and Karl is quite an accomplished golfer, about fifteen handicap, but he will be much lower than that when he gets experience and a lot of practice. Martin is slow but very flashy. He could have won a hundred tournaments but he didn't. Tell the truth of him though, he had a hundred excuses.

Roger's boys play mostly Ice Hockey. They are both very good at it. Killian, the eldest is a big guy, only seventeen, six foot two inches. He looks very impressive on the Ice. Speedy and skilful. He should go places. Tarin is a couple of years behind Killian, but he too is showing great promise. His chief characteristics are determination and dedication. He wouldn't let his brother away with anything, a great competitive spirit. Roger wasn't really the athletic type, that's my son, Killian and Tarin's dad. He also plays a bit of Hockey with the over forties, and was not bad at it. It was more of a social outing and get together rather than a tough competition. He too was a bit like Martin Murphy a bit slow but very flashy.

We will have to wait a few years now, at least four or five to see how they all fare out. God is good, and patience is a virtue.

I want to remind everybody, my son is the Ice Hockey coach of Boca High School, quite a bit of prestige goes with that title. They, (Boca High) started at rock bottom, probably the poorest team in their division, and I don't mean money, poor, I'm talking about talent, but now they have a very respectable win/lost average, and quite naturally a lot of credit goes to Roger. But he's the kind that likes a challenge. He's not the voice ferocious type. Like some coaches are, loud-mouths never get the most from their players, Roger prefers the psychological approach. You always get more with honey, than vinegar. He brings me to watch the Panthers. They are the professional team. His son Killian plays with the junior Panthers. Hopefully this association with the Panthers will lead to bigger and better things down the road.

Evan Murphy has ambitions of becoming a Pilot. To me that is a very exciting career. He is trying to get the appropriate de-gree in UCD (University College Dublin). We all wish him the best of luck and from what I hear, he is working hard. Keep the good work up Evan. Maybe we will fly with you in the future. I'm not sure if Karl will be as good as Rory McElroy, but he will be trying hard anyway. Good luck in your endeavours, what-ever they might turn out to be. We, Mona and I will be rooting for all of you, wherever you wind up in life.

Martin & Caroline Murphy's three children, Evan, Lauren and Karl

Majella is Roger's wife. Married in 1988 Roger and Majella work for the same company. They don't have to travel far. They have their own office in their own home. But they do travel occasionally, to different parts of the states on business matters. So far they have been very successful. They really have their daily routine organised to as near perfection as you could ever achieve. It really helps to be organised, when you have two jobs, and two boys going to two different schools. Where the boys go to school is not just around the corner, its a half hour each way morning and evening, and so far everything has worked like a Swiss watch. Boca High School, Killian – Tarin, St.Vincent Ferrer. They have to be at school at different times, and after that, on any given evening, hey have Ice Hockey in Coral Springs, forty five minutes each way. Some weeks, three games. You will agree that this is a tough schedule, week in week out. In bed at 11pm up at 7am. This is only for the young and ambitious. But at the same time, if you want something badly enough, you have to go after it.

Now I will talk about my Daughter Caroline and Martin's plans and fairly ambitious expectations from their children. As I said before Lauren is the eldest, and has her sights set on Pharmacy, but for the time being not permanently. She is side stepping Pharmacy to take what she hopes will be a stepping stone and get degree as a Lab. Technician, which she hopes will lead her successfully to a degree in Pharmacy. A lot of hard work and studying. Sorry, nose to the grind stone Lauren.

Evan, Caroline's oldest son, has his sights set on being a Pilot. He's studying in UCD Dublin for the appropriate degree to be an Airline Pilot. It's an ambitious outlook, and opens up many exiting places to fly to in a career as a Pilot. We will be praying to the great man above on your behalf. We wish you well and hope everything you hope for will come true, God willing. Karl is their youngest. Seventeen years old. He is a very good golfer. He won the Masters in Edenderry Golf Club in 2011.

Unfortunately the winters in Ireland are not golf friendly, with the result that the golfers play very little in the winter months, and that is a big disadvantage, especially the young golfers, who might have a lot of talent, but for lack of practice they don't develop their full potential, and it's like starting all over again when the winter is over. But there are people and you know them well and they are Irish, Rory McElroy, Graham McDowell, Padraig Harrington, Paul McGinley, Shane Lowry, our own Offaly man. The great Christy O'Connor Snr, and his nephew Christy O'Connor Jnr, and the world famous three wood he hit against none other than the great Freddie Couples, to win his match, in the Ryder Cup, will always be remembered. I suppose if you really have the talents, it's like cream, it will come to the top. Maybe I lit a spark under you Karl, and may the Good Lord will let it happen "Hallelujah". Caroline herself is no slouch. She runs for everything in Edenderry. She is better known than the Lord Mayor of Dublin a few years ago, Alfie Byrne. Come to think of it you should run to be Mayor, you'd skate in really, and they need a wakeup call in that town anyway. Paul Byrne would be your Deputy Mayor; John Delamere could be his advisor.

Left: Fr. Dan Moore, Killowen & Australia with Mona and I and our two children Roger and Caroline.

Right: My Mother when she visited New York in 1964

I will drop back to the years 1978, that's the year I got into business in New York. I got a partner who was also in the marble business, his name was Howard Fichtel. His father in law owned a small workshop also in New York, so Howie has some experience in the business. He was an easy guy to get along with. The marble shop we bought was in Long Island City. It was owned by two men, who happened to be retiring at that time, as a matter of fact I worked for them on many occasions. They were two nice gentlemen, and when they had a job to be done, I done it for them, they always gave me a call to see if I was available and depending on how good of job I had at the time determined my answer. I made nice money with those two. The same two gentlemen showed us and broke us in on how to use all the different blades and stone grits on all the cutters. The polishing process was strictly no water, just putty with acid, that spun at high speeds, the friction and heat developed the high shine and became polished marble.

What became a routine occurrence was our visits home, which were fairly often, especially when Caroline and Roger were in school in Ireland. We all looked forward to meeting and seeing each other. They were lovely homecomings, hugs and kisses and happiness all around. The children were a little older now, and were beginning to handle being away from home a little better. When Caroline got her holiday breaks from school, she usually came down the country to Edenderry, to Larkin's. Stasia Larkin was and is Caroline's aunt. But there were people who actually thought Caroline was one of the young Larkin's. Let me tell you, when you are three thousand miles away from your children, that is very reassuring. You would have to be in our situation to realize how much that meant to us, Mona and Denny. That's what I call the stuff of life. That is something you take with you all the way to the end of the road. Thank God it's now many years later and we're still the best of friends. Having said that let me hasten to add, that Eilish and all the Hoeys were also very good to Roger. Roger always recognizes that, and was always grateful for all the nice dinners he got in Hoeys, and also Kevin used to drive him back to Holy Faith in Newbridge. We don't, Mona and I forget all them favors' and are very thankful for them. Roger saw for the first time, a cow and a bull mating. Kevin told him that the cows and the bull were having an argument and the bull told her if she didn't behave he would have to chastise her and she did not behave, so he ran at her, and jumped up on her back, and prodded her with what looked like a big painted red carrot, and went away and left her then. He (the bull) looked like he was disgusted, but Kevin said that was only an act, that deep down he was delighted. That's what you're exposed to when your Aunt is a farmer. Back to Caroline again, I sent her a car, an automobile. I thought for three and a half thousand dollars, an Italian, they had a good reputation, but this was a real Lemon. The fellow I bought it from, said "you won't be sorry, Mr. McNamara, a great car, this is". Caroline got the car, well, it nearly broke her heart. You would never believe the trouble she had with it. She had to get rid of it. I was so sorry for doing that to Caroline. She had plans to pick up Roger in Newbridge now and again, that's where Roger went to School. I told her to dump it, and may all bad luck go with it. Caroline was starting to get fond of Edenderry. You see Stasia Larkin used to send her over to the Medical Hall, for little messages, and there was a cute little fellow working behind the counter. His name was Martin Murphy. Be God, if she didn't put her eye on him and that was the start of a romance that ended up at the altar.

I am just starting to work in the World Trade Centre, just working my day for other contractors. The Marble Contract was between fifteen or sixteen million dollars, with of course plenty of extras as the job progressed. The marble business like every other business was simply humming. There was a mass influx of workers arriving in the United States, in them years. Nobody in their wildest dreams ever though, the bubble would burst, or even more remote in anybody's mind that this magnificent building, that I and about two thousand other workers were putting together, would in, a few short years, be leveled, and almost three thousand people killed, masterminded by the most devious terrorist ever known to mankind. The United States will not give up in their quest to get him and all his accomplices, and I have no doubt some day they will.

Our people, the Marble Contractors, are usually the last trade, to complete on almost every job. You see its fragile, and the fewer other trades that remain the easier it is to store the marble, because there is more room and less danger of damaging the marble. In other words, it's great comfort and less nerve-racking. You might ask "What's all the fuss about". You have to understand the nature and composition of marble. For instance, the columns were matched columns, like you would match wallpaper. It took at least thirty million years for that marble to be in its present state. Can you imagine breaking one of them slabs, you would be up that same creek again, but this time without a paddle. That is exactly the reason, we insist on being the last trade on the job. As a Union Rep, that was part of my responsibility to make sure, or try, to be the last man standing, or the last trade on the job. We are getting down to the last few days on the job. This weekend will do it. There were sixty five lads under my jurisdiction. We will all be heading different directions. I know I'll be heading to Ireland with Mona and the two siblings, Caroline and Roger. I'll be only staying three weeks. Mona and the kids will probably stay at least eight or ten weeks. I enjoyed the stay in Ireland. A few pints in Larkin's, in Edenderry, an appetizer of course, and of course you can't beat the craic. Pat Larkin himself likes a couple of pints too. But he was I think a Budweiser man. I often drink Budweiser, but when I'm in Ireland I like to take advantage of the good pint of Guinness, it's a nice kind of high feeling. I feel a bit privileged to call myself and Mona a friend of Brian Cowen. I would get an argument going in a minute about that. Let me say this to the people who have an answer for everything, let me say, I'll be very brief – Tell me one country that has done well in this, the greatest and all encompassing depression. It has brought down every country in the world to its knees, including the great United States. Whoever thinks Brian Cowen was responsible for the downturn of the Irish economy needs to be rushed quickly to a head shrink. I could write an article on who really brought down the world economy; I would need a winding sheet to hold all the names. But I am not going down that road now.

At last the time has arrived for Mona and I, to send our children to school in Ireland, but because of a tragic death, of one of Roger's classmates, out mind was made up for us. This kid was twelve years old, what I am about to tell you is horrible. His name was Joe. Two people in balaclavas went to Joe's house, went to his bedroom. He was asleep. They turned him over on his stomach and shot him through the back of the head, and then disappeared into the night. The last time I enquired, the case was never solved. Awful sad, but it made up our minds, and it was school in Ireland for Roger and Caroline.

Caroline was fourteen years old, and when we were in Ireland that year, we brought her to Holy Faith in Glasnevin, Dublin. We had it all arranged, so all was set. That was our first goodbyes, and like all goodbyes, we were all lonely and sad. A few tears, last long looks from a distance. The next thing we are on a plane, the three of us, Roger, Mona and I. I have been on flights that we enjoyed more than this that was to be expected. It is now the year 1974, Roger has one more year at Our Lady of Angels School, a rather uneventful year, and we are planning for a return to Ireland. Roger would be making his debut in Christian Brothers, Newbridge.

Myself and my Son Roger

My son Roger with his wife Majella and their two sons, Killian and Tarin. Majella just got her masters degree in computer science.

Time passes quickly, and believe it or not, we are on our way back to Ireland again. This time of course, to bring Roger to college in Newbridge. We spent a good few days in Ireland. Tried to make Roger as happy as possible, but you could see he wasn't very happy. I was just thinking of myself, what kinds of a frame of mind have the people on death row. But to him I suppose he had all the troubles of the world on his shoulders. Believe me, it was just as hard on Mona and I to see him disappear into the dimly lit dorm, out of view, enough tears to go around, enough sadness to keep us very quiet for the next few hours. We will call into visit with Roger on the way back to Dublin. We were delighted to see he was mixing in great with the other young lads. There was this young lad from Cork, came up himself on the train to Kildare, and got a taxi out to Newbridge College. He said "I had to show your man (taxi driver) the money, I was so young, he said, he didn't think I'd have the money. I wouldn't blame him", he said. This kid, as the Cork men would say was "Tough Out". I was delighted he was going to be a friend of Rogers. "Don't worry Mr. & Mrs. McNamara, I will look after your son", he said. I tell you we left there happier that the night before, when we said goodbye to Roger. We headed to Dublin to visit with Caroline. She was delighted to see us naturally. The Reverend Mother was so nice, made us feel very welcome. Tea and Biscuits gratefully accepted, Caroline told us she had just got off the phone with Roger. He really has settled in, and now that she could get in touch with him by phone, made him feel better. The Reverend Mother told us Caroline was a rock of sense. "Anyway, not to worry about Roger, I will send him a couple of pounds, whenever he needs it", she said. You see we set Caroline up with a little account, Bank of Ireland, Edenderry, and with a little check book, of her own. All I said to her was. "If you ever write a check for more than a thousand, it will bounce". "What's bounce", she said. "It will be no good", I replied. "You don't have to have the slightest worry Dad, about that", Caroline replied. It was always easy saying goodbye to Caroline; she was always trying to comfort us.

We were up at the crack of dawn the next morning, and will soon be winging it back to New York. Another year has come and gone, always fairly eventful with us. Its 1975. Nothing ahead of us but work, what else is new. We spent a week off work, visiting with old friends; The Scanlon's were our neighbors forever. They had to be told all about the life and times of our children. They were really interested in all the stories. Like all our other old friends, The Casey's', Paddy, my good friend and his wife Joan. We got half loaded, re-hashing the old times, footballing days, and the children. We used to spend weekends up in Casey's in Rockland County, upstate New York. They were truly good old days. Pete and Patsy Nolan were also good friends of ours, and we met them regularly. It might be in Clara, Tullamore, or Edenderry, but theirs is a lifelong friendship. Also The Nolan's and the McNamara's, have almost the same lifestyle these days, and as far as I know neither of us are complaining.

I have great memories of some great weekends in the home of Paddy and Joan Casey, in Rockland, upstate New York, a few miles north of the Tappanlee Bridge. After dinner and a couple of drinks Paddy would play the tape of the All Ireland Final between Offaly and Kerry and of course the nightmare of Seamus Darby's goal that was sent ringing around Ireland. You could not blame the Kerry supporters for feeling so disgusted. With all the memorabilia marked so brightly, with the words "Five in a row", what heartbreak for them. But no game is over until it's over, so said a famous American baseball player, the one and only "Yoggi Berra".

Its twenty years ago since that game was played in Croke Park, something you might not know. The first All Ireland

Hurling (Senior) Final was played in Birr, County Offaly on Easter Sunday 1888. It was the 1887 final. Tipperary beat Galway by one goal and one point and a forfeit point to Nil. The Tynagh and Killimore members of the Galway team were unable to secure transport and walked to Birr. The All Ireland final of 1889 between Dublin (Kickams) and Clare (Tulla) was played at Inchicore, Dublin on 3rd November 1889 at a ground near the O'Blake Church, Tyreconnell Road, Dublin. Score 5-1 to 1-6. The Tulla men played barefoot in poor weather conditions. The first All Ireland football final was played at Clonskeagh, Dublin on the 29th April 1887, when Limerick commercials defeated Young Irelands of Louth. The ground at Beachill above the river Dodder between Donny and Clonskeagh is now covered by a housing estate.

I am drifting back now to pick up the story from, 1978 onwards. Caroline has one year to go in Holy Faith. Roger has two years to go in Newbridge, and I am about to start a business with a partner.

The business started to do nicely about 1980 and continued to do well into the late eighties. We had reached the stage, where we had up to seventy five people working for us. We needed financial stability. This is where I came in, and my Jewish partner was delighted that I was Irish and so we headed into New York, to the Bank of Ireland, and got introduced to the manager, Bill Burke. A very nice man all the way from Co. Mayo. I had been speaking to him on the phone so he knew what we wanted and more importantly he knew what he wanted, all the ongoing jobs and all the new jobs with the signed contracts. He spent a considerable time looking at all the paperwork with his accountant. "Well gentlemen", he said, "Myself and my accountant have agreed that you are indeed doing very well and now we have to discuss what line of credit you are asking for".

So I said, with the permission of my partner, "you fellows know figures, in all likelihood better than we do, and we would be willing to accept your recommendation, for a trial period, let's say one month". Bill Burke replied with a grin on his face, "Done and dusted, one hundred thousand a week", he said, "That should be sufficient". And it was. It's another year on now, Caroline is finished Holy Faith, and I alone went to Ireland. Mona didn't come, she will later. I get the job of socializing for a very short stay. Roger comes back with me. He starts working a little bit in the factory. He is learning fast. More importantly for him, he is saving a few bucks. Roger and I nosh it up together, no cooking at home in the house now. Mona is on her way to Ireland, actually landed there today. Caroline will be happy now. This all took quite a bit of planning, don't you think.

When Roger and Caroline were in school and even long after that, we made a lot of trip back to Ireland, as a matter of fact Caroline remained permanently in Ireland. She married, the sweetheart friend from her school days. They built a nice bungalow type home on her husband's property, just one hundred yards from the Medical Hall; we call them drug stores in the States. They also converted Martin's mother's bungalow, into a beauty parlor which Caroline runs with the help of a couple of girls. Martin also extended his properties, with a few shops that are doing business. I don't have to tell anybody about the sagging economy as is the rest of the countries at this point in time, but there are glimmers of hope appearing on the horizon. By and large the world's economy is still in recession, and will still take time to recover. I doubt it will ever reach what it was in the "Celtic Tiger" days. People around the world will have to tighten their belts and get used to a slightly lower standard of living. To be honest, when I look around me, at the average person, they look like they are not hurting or hungry to me; on the contrary they look prosperous and well fed. The United States is not nearly recovered yet. The business is going good, all the guys that work for us are good workers, and know what is expected of them. They are well paid, and are expected to produce the goods, which I must say, so far have.

We took on a big contract in New Jersey. New Jersey is a state, just like New York is a state. To work in any other state, would mean long journeys cost money, but New Jersey is just on the other side of the Washington Bridge and from there, only three miles up the Palisades Parkway, was where we had the big contract. Myself and my partner were out at the site doing some measurements, which is a necessary pre-requisite, to ordering the big panels of Travertine, it's just simple mathematics, when you have the overall length of the walls, which we enter on the architectural drawings. The drawings are sent, in this case to Italy, to their quarry we use for Travertine all the time. The drawings require the architect's signature guaranteeing the measurements. Not all that simple my friends. While we were taking the measurements, there was this "chubby chap", taking a great interest in what we were doing. So one word borrowed for another, he got chatting to us. He looked at the details on the architectural drawings. "How do you fellows propose to attach those bolts to the steel", he asked. We informed him that we bought an automatic electric welder. It kind of astounded him. He figured us for a couple of dummies. That might have been a slight mistake on his part. Then he told us something we already knew, the steel work and welding is the jurisdiction of the Ornamental Iron Workers Union, and so we said, "No problem, do you know any good man that you could recommend to us". "I do", he said, "His name is John McDonagh". So we asked him if he was on this job at present, which he was. "Will you introduce us to him", we asked. "You're talking to him", he said, and I said "You re-hired as the welder on this job". "My name is John McDonagh, but with one stipulation, I'm known as "Big John". "Ok," I said,

"Your Big John from now on, and more importantly, your Hired".

Well with Big John on board, we will take on the world. Not really, but it's a plus to have his experience on your side. Howie and I will spend a week out here in Palisades laying out this job. The big Travertine job; and then in a couple of weeks or so, I will bring Big John out to put up some permanent lines. We will use Piano wire for those lines. They will be so taught that you can hear a musical tone from them when you touch them. That's why they call it Piano Wire. The wire will be set on a steel post on both corners, and it will reflect the height and the face of the Travertine panels. So that when the stone setter sets his panels, all he has to do is follow those lines with the Travertine panels. Now before the stone setters, as there will be a few of them, Big John and his assistant will be well ahead of them, with the welding of the bolts to the main steel structure. It will be a few weeks before the Travertine arrives from Italy, maybe ten or twelve. The welding will be completed very soon. I am sending Big John into Manhattan to run a big job we have there. The Republic National Bank and that will take about a year to complete and after that we have the Marriott hotel, 47th street and Broadway, probably another year to complete. We also have lots of small jobs on the side. With fifty workers or up to one hundred at peak times.

You now realize the importance of Mr. Bill Bourke, Bank of Ireland, Fifth Avenue, manager. The Republic Bank is going strong. Payday for the men was Thursday. I usually brought the checks about 2.15pm, so they could change them before the bank closed, but I heard a little rumor that they ducked out of the job at 11.30am instead of 12pm.(12pm to 12.30pm was Lunch break). I came early with the checks purposely at 1.30pm, nobody on the job. I was fairly fuming. The bar was next door, so I went in immediately and caught them red handed, drinking on my time. Now nobody would mind a few minutes, but some of them were there two hours – Big John the ring leader. I told him they are here with your permission, you gave them permission. He tried to tell me he promised them an hours drinking if they produced a certain amount of work. So I said to him "I won't say it any more, a repeat performance, and you and all these men are all gone, every single one of you including Big John, OK". I went into the bar man afterwards. He was an Irish lad. He told me that they were doing that for a long time, not all of them but most of them. He said, "I told the three or four guys that didn't drink, why didn't they get word out to me. They said they were afraid to get involved". So what I did, was give the bar tender, my phone number, and if they are in there drinking, to give me a call. "You know their names; you change most of their checks". "I will", he said, "and what about me", he said. I did take care of him. I notice whenever I visit the job now, which is at least once a week, I seem to be getting much more respect. But I have to say, we are making progress and that by any equation is the name of the game. Not the end of the world.

It won't be long now until Roger is back for the summer break. Howie is busy in the Shop, keeping abreast of all the drawings and blue prints. We have a permanent draughtsman, a nice little man, Hungarian by birth. I spend many a day measuring with him and then back to his office to review them, and we have a nice sandwich and a glass of wine, prepared by his housekeeper. I'm heading home now, I drive through Manhattan, on to the Major Deegan Expressway, exit at Vancortland Park exit, and then to my condominium. Mona beat me home for a change and will be preparing dinner. Roger will be here next week; we are always looking forward to him arriving. He will be looking for full wages now. He is finished in NewBridge. He is very good at setting the marble. He will be going to the Marriott Hotel. That a big job and he will spend his summer break there; looking for Big Bucks'. He had a girlfriend now. When he goes back to Dublin, Stephens Green actually, a Business school, he will be trying for a degree in Business Administration. We are now almost seven years in business, and we are doing fairly good. The outlook is pretty good also. This coming Fall, about October, I am being honored by the Offaly Men's Association. Well I did give quite a few Offaly guys a break, from the following places; Tullamore – four lads, Birr area – three or four lads, including the Offaly Hurling Fullback we christened him "The Jolly Green Giant", Rhode – five or six, Edenderry a few, including "The Ginger", a few Dubs and also Northern Ireland – one or two lads. One or two from most of the counties from time to time, I nearly did hire from every county. A few Americans – nine or ten, American Irish, American Italian and other nationalities as well. I tried to be fair, to everybody money wise, they did better with us than any of the other companies they worked for. They all would agree to that. Time is flying, the summer is gone and Roger is on his way back to Ireland. Can't wait to get back to the girlfriend, who is from Dublin. Her name, by way of introduction is Majella Boylan, a stunning blond. I think she has him fairly well hooked. No more sad faces going back to Ireland. Thank God, what time can do? But also a lot of worry has disappeared from my own and Mona's lives. Up to now there was a big void in our lives, without both Caroline and Roger, but Thank God, the stress and strain has practically diminished. Caroline is happy, doing her time that it takes to qualify to be a Nurse. Roger will not be coming to the Offaly Man's Association dance honoring me. It just wouldn't make sense, he will only be gone back about two weeks. I understand, plus he would be leaving the honey bunch after him being away from her all summer. We are fairly sure, he won't come and we will respect his decision gladly.

Well its now the evening before the big night, and we are expecting somebody, we don't really know who. We have a driver out there with the big station wagon. We are getting a little anxious; at last the door bell rings. Caroline was only one shown, and then in about five minutes the bell rings, and who was it only the bold Pat Larkin, needless to say we knocked back a few that night.

Now it was time to get ready for Big Night, we were all decked out in our finest, we had a few cocktails before we left to the big bash held in the Astoria Manor, all such occasions are always booked out and this was no exception. The head table of course was reserved for the guest of honor the chairman of the Offaly Men's Association, then me and special guests, the crowd in general would be at least seventy percent Offaly people, but a good representation from most other counties, that would be standard procedure. As far as I was concerned all were important people in their own right but I would have to give the vote to the man himself, Bank of Ireland manager New York's, Bill Bourke. I said that in my speech and evidently he was important to other people in the audience as well because he got a thundering applause. You often heard that old cliché that money talks and shit walks and that is as true today as it ever was, Jackie Gleeson used to say, the loneliest feeling in the world is an empty pocket. In my young days, most people in Ireland had that lonely feeling.

Getting back to the big night, it was a huge success and the speeches were mind boggling. I never thought I was such a nice guy, I was a nervous wreck, gutted, staggered through the speech, got through it one way or another. I was never as happy as when it was over. I was very impressed with the candor and the sincere thanks of the people who worked for me over the years, I met people from all parts of Ireland, but the majority was from Offaly. What I was particularly proud of was Caroline, my daughter, got to say a few words. I awarded her the Oscar for the night; one thing she always had was a gift of the gab and never lost it. You very often hear accolades about people after they pass away, but one is seldom a prophet in his own time, a lot of us are legends in our own mind, its part of being human. There was several people that paid me nice compliments, I don't remember all of them, or do I, I'll try my best and give you my best shot, Bill Bourke, Frank Feighery, Pat Fluery, Oliver Delany, Pat Larkin, Paddy Mc Cormack, Willie Lowry. I take this opportunity to thank all of them very much for their kind remarks. Bill Bourke might get that Oscar there. Moving on from that affair, there are very big celebrations in the offering, a monumental one, The Centenary of the Offaly Men's Association, I heard from the grapevine that there will be a big contingent of Offaly people at it. They are making plans already, Mona said she is fully booked for the occasion, in our humble, three bed, two bathroom condo, when it's a celebration of that magnitude, you have to stretch a point. It's nice to have your friends around; Mona is a little more pragmatic, she says "company is like fish, after three days it smells". I'll get back to that part of the story a few weeks later.

Some of the most enjoyable trips we have done over the years were trips with the grandchildren, to Disneyland in Orlando. We had the full complement of relatives, Mona and I had our grandchildren, and Rodger and Majella had Majella's sister Ashling, her husband Niall and their children. I think altogether there were eleven of us. We rented a double apartment, there were five bedrooms and believe me, you needed the space, especially when the kids fell out. I almost forgot about Caroline and Martin; they rented next door to us, another two bed roomed, two bathroom apartment. Between us we almost had the whole complex. That eleven turned out to be sixteen, we all enjoyed it, especially for the kids sake, we all had to look happy anyway. We all went out to the restaurant for the first evening for dinner that happened to be the last evening we went out to dinner; it was not our grandchildren's finest moments so from there to the end it was take away, "big time"! The children were happier back in the apartments and we had no hassle, a few drinks and great food, and as the younger ones fell of asleep and put to bed, we lived it up. Right next door was the liquor store, and beer. So where would you be going with no bell on your bike, Martin Murphy was off the beer for a week. Would you believe that, but somebody said he drank three bottles of gin, but he did put some tonic and ice into it, and they were saying wasn't Martin great to be off the beer, Ashling said to Niall "you should follow Martin's example". I would but I can't afford it. All in all we had a memorable week, one of the many we had in Orlando, if we had any little complaint it would be the weather, ninety five degrees, its lethal. Over the years we had a lot of visitors, mostly to New York, on a few occasions P.J McEvoy (Rev.), always a great laugh, jokes a plenty mostly very clean of course and another one of our well know friends Jack Welsh and his wife, Rita, they really enjoyed themselves and it was nice to have them. They have both left the Building. Jack was a legend in his own time. Loved a little drop. Jack went to every funeral in the country, at least the ones that were no more than forty miles away. He would say of a particular funeral that was the best funeral I was ever at, Jack would stay for the afters, long after. The way he evaluated a funeral was the amount of drink that was available.

I happened to be driving behind a car today. They are great for funny stickers on the back of cars. This one read, 'are you married or are you happy'. He exited that street and I am behind a different car, and his sticker read, 'Jesus loves me, how come everyone else calls me an asshole'. I thought they were funny.

In the meantime another year has passed and this is the year of the big Centenary celebrations, and the Offaly Association will be making history as well as the Hurlers and Footballers and all the airwaves will be busy. Literally bringing people from many countries. Offaly are, according to my sources of information, are the oldest Irish association in New York. Six weeks to go and we will storm the banquet hall.

Our marble business is going pretty strong and so was the Celtic Tiger. At that time in history, Big John is still on board, with his wings slightly clipped. We didn't have a call from the barman, you remember the bar next door, to the Republic National Bank. The workers realized I was serious, when I said a repeat of drinking on my time was not on, so that situation was taken care of. Of course you never know until a job is completed how well you have done. Sometimes some extras appear and you can make nice profits. These are items that were not originally anticipated. All contractors love the extras. No outside bidders for extras and you can let in the needle a little bit.

Like I said, it's another year on, and we are now about to start in the Marriott. We signed the contract. I haven't mentioned my partner very much, you see he takes care of the office and factory, and I take care of the jobs wherever they are. We have a job we just signed in New Haven, Connecticut, a nice sized job, and a bigger one in Stanford, also in Connecticut. We have about four years work on the books at present. So getting the jobs is not a problem. Doing them is more of a problem. You see to run a job you have to have experience, and know what you are doing. They are the ones that are scarce. They get whipped up like hot cakes. Both the Connecticut jobs are a year away, which means a little breathing space, to arrange for Mona and I to come separately. This way we are prolonging our time with Roger and Caroline.

I am back now, and will be going from job to job keeping an eye on things and at times, that is very essential. I'm five or six months back now and we are progressing along good. It's amazing how many Irish lads are here in New York. All you have to do is go into any of the leading bars at lunchtime, Irish bars of course, there is almost nothing else. The most popular one was the Blarney Stone. They were three Irish lads that owned this bar. You should see those bar tenders move, like robots, you would think, they had an electric plug in their rectum. There was a two hour lunchtime, from noon until two o'clock, The bosses told those young barmen, "If you can't move quick enough, there is somebody right outside the counter ready to take your place", They moved. Time and tide waits for no man, a very true saying. Low and behold, Roger is back again. Nothing on his mind, only money. Mona will be in Ireland for a few weeks to be with Caroline, as much as possible. Roger will be heading to the Palisades' in New Jersey, remember that one, The Travertine has arrived in the port of New York and we are making arrangements to have it delivered to the job. No messing there. The Teamsters Union handles that end of it. Expensive, but it will get to the job safe and sound, and worry free for us; they are a big plus, two thousand tons of it.

You might be interested to know where the Travertine came from. It comes foaming down from the top of the burning mountain, in the form of molting lava. It looks to the naked eye, a sea of red fire. After about a couple of months, it cools out, it starts in the bowels of the earth with a heat that is inexplicable, and it literally belches that molten lava up through the mountain and roaring down to the flat earth below. Its when it cools out, the big machinery moves in, and that equipment makes it into big cubes, roughly ten feet long by five feet wide, by five feet deep, about two hundred and fifty cubic feet. These cubes are taken to a factory that has all the machinery to handle their size. In any case we ordered the slabs the exact size the architects called for, so when we get them on the job, they are a perfect size. The job begins; we have a stone mason that is supposed to be qualified to install this Travertine. Let me tell you first of all, that Big John and I spent three days putting the piano wire in one hundred percent the right place, both for height and also the face. The wire served two purposes. The Height and The Face. The job was started, was about three days in progress, so I said, I'll check to see how they are doing. When I got close to where they were working, I saw a lot of cut pieces. I fumed, I didn't say a word for about a half an hour, and then I told Roger, my son to tell this man, who had the balls to call himself a stone setter to pack his bags and not to stop running until he gets back to wherever he came from. So my son told him he was fired. "But I want my money", he told Roger. Luckily I had a check book with me and he was on his way. I never knew where he came from, as a matter of fact, I found out later he was recommended by a friend of Big Johns. I'm not sure if he was or not. The damage is done and he is gone. I have to get into this screw up. I'm out there brave and early on Monday morning. The damage done will cost about forty thousand dollars. But that is not the end of the world. Luckily it's Travertine and luckier still none of the pieces that were cut off from the panes were broken. They are all in one piece, and still more luck, it will be relatively easy to find the matching pieces for each panel. By the evening, we set them up on flat crates, put all the panels on the crates and Roger and another kid started to match them, it took hours. Next day we will Akemi them back together. It's tomorrow now. The big operation starts. By the way we have plastic shims one sixteenth of an inch between the panels and the crates, if you didn't you'd be in real trouble. I mix the Akemi, all is ready, we have to work quickly, and we are doing half today and the rest tomorrow. Roger is good at this; he has experience from the shop. He applies the Akemi to the edges. I myself will do the actual sticking. It's going beautiful, we have exactly half of what we are sticking today done, the other young lad was doing great, I showed him how to get the excess Akemi off the panels. He picked up right away; he waited a couple of minutes before peeling the glue off, it came out perfect. Tomorrow I will put the finishing touches on that, and if you didn't know, where those cuts were made you would never find them. How about that for a bit of skill. The next day, we repeated the same thing, another lovely job. Finished that part of the project, it was Friday evening, and it was back to Casey and Byrne's Pub to relax and have a few drinks. The phone rings.

The barman answered the phone. We had a nick-name on the barman, Big Dog, Big Dog said to me "are you still here Denis?" he had his hand covering the phone, "No", I said. He said "that was the war department. She said dinner's on the table". So we threw them down, and left the drinks, that is. I remember she told me to bring a couple of loaves and a pound of sliced ham, she was expecting a couple of friends later for a few drinks. We (Roger and I) landed in, loaves and ham, and a couple of shit eating grins on us. "You are lucky you thought of the messages or you would have got no dinner", she said. Peace broke out, and we had a great dinner and a great old chat and a couple of more beers. It's amazing what can happen all in the space of one day.

Back to the Marriott Hotel, and now I am making a switch in the team. Big John will now run the Travertine Job in New Jersey, the one we just fixed all the cut panels in. I don't have to tell you John about the Piano wire, or anything else about the job, you and I put that wire in place, but just to see that everything will go alright, I went there for a few days, and John I said, the only thing that critical, now you got to watch is on the very first panel, make sure you stay up from the steel in the bottom, at least five eighth of an inch. So he is clear about that. I'll be here anyway. We had a beautiful hoist on the big rubber tires. The panels were all standing up against big columns, you just put the clamp on top, tighten it well, and away you go to the edge of the building. Now it hovers into position, five eighth shims under it, edge is plumbed, face is plumb, tighten bolts. Before we cement the side anchors we lower the next panel into position, shims under, looking real good. The height perfect. The face plumb, cement them up and we were on our way again, after a rough start. Goodbye John, you are on your own. I'm out of here, just one more thing John; check the measurement out to the end now and again, so that we finish with the same full panel. That would be fairly critical John. "I understand that would be", he agreed. "We got off to a bad start John, not your fault, but push it a little if you can. See you in a few days John", I replied.

The Old Republic Bank I have neglected for a couple of weeks now. But I stay right on top of them almost every day. I am looking forward to a visit from Caroline. We no doubt take her around some interesting places, like Downtown Manhattan, Saks 5th Avenue, Macys Department Store, where her mother Mona actually worked. Mona will show her the very counter she worked at, a slight touch of nostalgia there. Maybe a tear or two. It certainly will bring back memories. I worked for a couple of months there myself. Selling ladies high heel shoes. "Get this", at ninety-nine cents a pair. I sold one thousand, eight hundred pairs the first day. I was like a Jack in a Box, I did some fancy moves, but you may or may not believe this, the man who had the stall rented, gave me fifty dollars and forty dollars wages on top of that. People in a big hurry leaving the change that would be small change. They would just say with a wave of the hand, keep it. It came to twenty seven dollars. I had a lovely day, one hundred and seventeen dollars. But that was just a once off. That was what they call here, a close out sale, everything had to go. Tomorrow it will be dry bread and buttermilk. I happened to be in the right place at the right time. Mona, Caroline and I went to lunch at Mike Carty's Place, 51st and 7th avenue, Manhattan. Rosie O'Gradys was the name of the place; it was a pub restaurant type, mega business going on there, couldn't happen to a nicer guy. I have been there several times. If anybody is coming out from

Ireland, don't forget to pay it a visit. You will be well taken care of. Tell Mike, Denis McNamara sent you.

Myself, Mona, Leo O'Dowd and Ann, often had dinner there and a couple of drinks also. Brings back to Mona and I very happy memories of very happy times. Leo O'Dowd and Ann live now in a beautiful home in Connemara, Co. Galway. It's just outside Galway City. They are very happy there and Mona and I visit them every year. We look forward to it. We never have a drink when we meet them, would you believe, that, of course, you wouldn't and you'd be right.

I better get back to Caroline, because she is only here for a week or maybe ten days. So we try to cram in as much as we can for that short stay, the last time she came she brought her son Karl. He had a ball with Roger's two boys; they played Golf almost every day. The three of them played at different courses and I joined them, a couple of times. The weather was warm, but we had the Golf Buggies. The kid's loved driving the buggies, doesn't all young lads. Killian and Karl had great fun to see who could hit the drives the longest. The contest was fairly even. They both hit it long. When Killian caught this long drive I said "Oh my God, I don't go that far on my holidays". They got a laugh out of that. Caroline and Karl are out of time. We are on our way to the airport. In all the goodbyes we've had over the years, we still get a bit lonely when members of the family are leaving or even friends. But that is human, and it always happens.

Back to work now, I not sure which direction to go. I'll head out to New Jersey to visit Big John. I was kind of disappointed with the progress, and I let Big John know that. He got very pissed off, and said "would you like me to quit?" "No I wouldn't want you to quit but at the same time, suit yourself", I replied. "Ok", he said, "But I don't want you coming around telling me we're slow". I replied "No I won't be coming around, I am going to stay here, and see if we can step up production". But I am not going to bore you with the details of the system, and nobody was overworked. To be brief, we got ten panels ready, plugs, anchors, everything ready for the hoist. One hour it took with everybody doing something instead of the helpers standing there pulling their plunker watching the setters doing the whole thing. We set the ten panels the same day, and let me tell you, they were on the job ten days, and had thirty panels set, and according to very simple mathematics that was three panels a day, and Big John had the balls to get mad when I said, I was a bit disappointed, in fact I was very disappointed but I will let the John sum up his own thoughts on that one. I said to John, "I am not going to stay a couple of weeks like I said, but I'll be back in a couple of weeks, in which time I will decide if you are going to be working for us". He didn't like that. "Ok Denis", he said. A lot has happened in that couple of weeks, some of which you might get it hard to believe. We had two brothers working for us from Mayo. They were hardy lads; they would go anywhere and do anything. They had their own pickup truck. They would chop concrete floors; make crates for shipping jobs, anything at all. No problem to those two lads. One evening as they did before, they stopped into a bar in Queens, and there happened to be a soccer game on television. Ireland versus Hungary, I'm pretty sure. They got in an argument with a guy at the bar, a customer just like themselves. An argument started, silly old stuff, Ireland are tougher than those Hungarians. They were trying to get your man to throw a punch, but he was too smart. He wouldn't take on the two of the (Folans), Seamus and Pat, and I'll tell you, he would be dead right. But Lo and Behold, who came through the door, he was about half an hour away, only the Hungarian. He walked up behind them, pulled out a gun and shot the two of them in the back of the head. They were dead before they hit the floor. O, what a tragedy. I was absolutely stunned. We had to get out there and identify them. I was never a shook in my whole life. Also that guy might come back and shoot whoever was there in sympathy for them. I have never forgotten it, over the years. They were two nice lads, great workers; you hadn't to stand watching them. May the Lord Have Mercy on them, we took care of everything.

So I said I'd see John in a couple of weeks, it's actually three weeks (fifteen working days). To be honest, judging from the way they worked before the argument, this was very good. They had one hundred and thirty five panes installed since I was here. So naturally I complimented John. I knew by the condescending grin in him, he had something on this mind. "I was hoping you would take me off this one now", he said. Why would I do that when this one is going so well? "I'd like to get to the Marriott Hotel, because there is going to be hoisting engineers working there for you, and they are notorious. They would do nothing if they got away with it, everybody knows that", John said. "I will consider that John", I replied. After some negotiations, we got away with two engineers. They make about two hundred and fifty dollars per day. God forbid, there would be any overtime. I got my partner in on this one, and we made a firm agreement to all concerned. The decision now is, do we bring Big John to the Marriott Hotel job, he can be very persuasive, and we really need that here. I'm on my way, and I'm betting to myself that the production won't have dropped down, simple logic, for that is John wants to stay in my good books. It's actually nine working days since I last visited, so I am figuring eighty panels that would be the same average as before, as a matter of fact, they had exactly eighty one done. Very good again. I was satisfied with that. So I said, well done
John. He asked me, had we decided if he was going to the Marriott Hotel. "Yes, you'll be going there." I replied. You know

what, he was like a dog with two tails, so when I was leaving, I told him," a week from next Monday you won't forget John?". "I certainly won't, I'll meet you there are 7.30am, on 12th June." He replied.

The Republic National Bank is nearly finished. I think the lads that worked there might be thinking of getting dried out, but really I think they might have learned a lesson. The job came out looking good, and I think we will make a few bucks on it. Roger will soon be back for two or three months. He will be headed to the Marriott Hotel. Howie's son wanted to work with him but we sent him to New Jersey. We also knew he won't do anything but harm. He's as useless as tits on a bull; at least he's out of the way.

This is Monday morning. Big John is here already at the Marriott. The marble work has begun there. Big John and I are looking at the outside; it's really unusually easy to start. We will be setting the first course on a Terrazzo base. We just have to take a starting point. The architectural drawings and we are all set. It takes a couple of days to get organized, with tools and tool boxes and picking a good big room, for the workers to change in. That will be our headquarters until the job is completed, about a year from now. Almost ready to move the troops in there now. So we are off and running at the Marriott. We did a very thorough preparation and hopefully with the help of God everything will turn out OK.

The Centenary Celebration is with us. Mona and I have our full quota of visitors, after all we have limited space, three bedrooms, two bath roomed condo. Our close friends of course will be with us. It will be helter skelter for a long weekend and because it's an Irish affair, there will be no drinking. You can swallow that, with a grain of salt. The booze is all in place, the whole works. We arrive at the banquet hall, all spit and polish. The ladies are all dressed in stunning full length gowns, and the men in tails. This is not just any old celebration. This looks like a fashion exhibition, "Saks Fifth Avenue". The music is by the famous, Glen Miller Orchestra.

The M.C for the night is the very articulate Frank Feighery. So the first dance is called, and the tune is an old time waltz, Mama Coyne's favorite, the famous, Blue Danube, and everybody is out on the floor. The waiters are very busy bringing to the tables, the best vintages of Red and White wines. There are also spirits, whatever the guests ask for, nothing spared. The Toast was for all the members past and present, and good wishes and thanks to all the visitors. Everybody, that is that's drinking, has had a couple and are really feeling over the moon, and enjoying every minute of it. As the meal is starting to be served, there is a choice of Roast Beef Fillet Mignon, Lamb, Pork or Salmon, will all the trimmings. The craic is mighty, you can hear the fun and laughter coming from all tables, and it's really true, the old song, "When Irish Eyes are Smiling", all the world is bright and gay, we are a light-hearted race. We are well after the time agreed on to finish the celebrations, but the management reps agreed to continue for one more hour. The guests were absolutely delighted, after all they reasoned, this only happens once every one hundred years. We might as well take advantage of their kind offer, because I don't think we will attend the next one. The dancing only really got going for this last hour. The curtain at last was drawn down, on one of the most enjoyable nights. We were all headed in different directions, to where would you think, back to all our social watering holes. We all headed back to Casey & Byrnes. The ring-leader Paddy Casey, my good friend. We stayed there to the wee hours, about five am in the morning. I can tell you, we were all fairly looped. There were five or six in my place; I think nobody was awake five minutes after we went in the door. They just wanted to sleep. I was checking the door, and there was dead silence, except for the odd funny but familiar old sounds!

It's now nine in the morning. Still not a sound, but ten am came, and somebody came shuffling out, Pat Larkin. "How are you feeling Pat?", "Not bad, I thought I would be worse", he replied. Mona has the breakfast leaping, in the two pans. Bacon, eggs, sausages (Irish, the only kind). We had a hearty breakfast, chatted, and they had some friends pick them up, five of them, went out to be shown around the city. Pat Larkin stayed with us, as he was family. Pat married Mona's sister, Stasia. We did our own thing, Mona and Stasia went shopping, Pat and I went shopping the Irish Pubs and really that's all there is. We visited a couple of Martin Griffins' pubs, Pat and I played golf with him a couple of times. A Mayo man, very successful in the States, basically New York., has six pubs. The one we went to, his famous one, The Jug of Punch. We had a few halers there with Martin, and then back home. The two women were in just ahead of us, more cocktails, and then a light dinner. The boys were invited to stay with a couple of other families; it took the pressure off, although we didn't mind. We chatted into the night, with a little Baileys; we enjoyed it immensely going back over old times. Pat and Stasia came to us on their honeymoon. We met them that time at the Airport. We were driving home from the airport, and Pat said, "I'll tell you one thing Mack, money fucking melts", he was amazed at the size of everything. I cracked up laughing, consider, he's only coming in from the airport. I'm saying to myself, he mustn't have a whole lot if it in his pocket. Continuing on about Pat, our neighbor, a lovely Cork woman, and married to a very nice man, Brendan and May Scanlon was their names, May bought Pat a nice looking shirt and tie, a present. It was too small for Pat, so Mona told them, she would get the sales slip from May and brings the shirt and tie back to the store, and gets their money back. "A great idea", said Stacia with the little scarcity of money, this will boost the kitty.

So off they went brave and early Monday morning. Stacia told the lady, "We're returning a shirt and tie, where do we line up?" the lady replied, "Right here, follow those people on this line". Lo and Behold there were at least forty people in front of them. Two hours in line, one person up front handling this crowd. Well they were about to collapse by the time they reached their turn. But the lady said, "No problem, a full refund", but when she handed them ninety nine cents, Stacia said, "Let's go around the corner and collapse". When they came back much later than expected and told us the story, we had the laugh of a lifetime. Pat said, the only way to get over this, is a few drinks, and some good food. Mona got on the phone, and booked dinner for four at the Coach and Four Restaurant, 262nd Stone Broadway as seven o'clock. The boys are not coming back tonight, staying with other friends, as we head up to the Coach and Four to dinner. No nicer or decenter man, than the owner, a Cavan man, Joe Coryning. It's also a very well know restaurant. His wife a delightful hostess, seated us at the best table, it's elevated, and looks down on all the guests. I introduced Pat and Stacia to Joe and told him, they were on their honeymoon. "Oh isn't that lovely, I will be back in a minute", Joe said, and he came back with a bottle of Dom Perignon. "That's on me", he said. I was a good customer of Joes, Mona and I went there at least once a week and often twice. Another happy memory.

They are all staying in our house tonight. Mona is cooking a farewell dinner. I am driving them all back tomorrow morning, in the big Ford Station Wagon. We are in Kennedy Airport and no doubt they all had an unforgettable week and four days. We were delighted to have them, and like the song says, "We'll meet again, don't know where, don't know when, but we will meet again somewhere, Goodbye".

Its time to get back to the Marriott, we're starting this morning to actually start installing the granite and the marble. We have a full complement of workers, a little pep talk, and we're on our way. I spoke specifically to the two derrick men, (derrick men were hoisting engineers) and I leveled with them, I said, "I don't know if you know it or not, but you guys haven't the best reputation of being great workers". Their reply would be fairly typical from a derrick man. "We don't want to be great Mr. McNamara; we just want to be paid every week". I wasn't about to get into any confrontation with them, I just walked away. Maybe a little honey instead of vinegar might be good. These guys could make you or break you because production depends on them. They handle and put in place every slab of granite from the stone masons to set, if they dog it, it would be very bad news for me. I never asked Big John how they did it, but I slipped a hundred spot, in each of their first pay packets. I was there about the middle of the next week, and I just said to John, "How are those derrick men doing?", and he told me, they were good workers; they keep them slabs going up there. There seems to be good harmony between them and the stone masons. I'm liking what I'm, hearing. My biggest nightmare is becoming a daydream. My son is up on the eighth floor, doing very well setting a rotunda, a complete circle. Howie's son tried to get in with him, a real arrogant bastard. They had an argument, Roger landed a haymaker on his chin, knocked him off the scaffold, I thought we were in a spot of trouble, but we were saved by the bell, he was on probation, so he couldn't even mention it, or he would have to go before the Probation board.

He never came back near the job, everybody was happy about that, so was his father, who kept him away somewhere, nobody, enquired where!

There are seven hundred and fifty bathrooms in the Marriott. As there is a lot of cutting and fitting, we can use one helper, for the two guys that are installing. They have the system down pat, as they are all identical bathrooms. When they got the first done, they follow that right to the last one. They are getting two bathrooms a day completed. It will take them three hundred and fifty days. The management might push us for three more men that would cut the time in half. That would be no problem. If we have to we'll just bring another crew. The fun is going to be later on with the surround of the circular bar. That circular wall will be four foot high, tile on each side, (that's marble tile) and one foot wide tile for the cap, all exposed edges polished. The brains were all working on this project. I told Jimmy Guinan what was going on, but not to say anything about it to anyone, that's a couple of months away, so we won't worry about it now, just to say it's a very big circle. The bar itself will be circling at one inch every five minutes; you definitely can't detect its movement. But let's say you were having a meal with a few friends and a drink, you could spend two or three hours, you could have moved three feet, all of a sudden, that big building you were keeping an eye on, is gone, you would probably think you were getting over the top, it's a very interesting concept, and I am for one am looking forward to having a meal at it when we have the surround marbleized, and its open for business. But that's down the road a little bit. This job is progressing nicely. The job in Hartford Connecticut is getting close, too close for comfort. If we get too jammed with work we could always sub-let it to another marble company. We did that before and it worked out alright. A few lads got laid off recently, but if they are still out of work in two or three weeks, we might like some of them back. Out in the building sites, the Union controls that end of it. About two months from now, The Republic Bank will be finishing, and a few more might bite the dust. I have a good idea who the ringleaders were, on those drinking binges, you remember that, and we got it sorted out. But I'm sure there will be a bit of "Lickus Tuckus" now with a couple of weeks to go, nobody likes to be laid off. They don't know it, but we will have a space for most them, the only couple that will hit the dust will be the two ringleaders, but the ones that went along for the ride are almost as guilty. So we will play it by ear for now.

I got letters from some of the Centenary people. They said that they never enjoyed anything like the time they had in New York. We were delighted, and did all we could to make it the memorable week for them.

The Marriott is three months on now, we started the surround. Two key men on that, Jimmy Guinan, and my son Roger. You remember I said there were all kinds of suggestions on how to do it, but Guinan and I threw them all out. The only real problem was the Cap. But we found out the best way was to leave out every second tile. Common sense prevailed. All we had to do then was measure accurately in between the set ones, and it worked like a dream perfectly. The supposedly huge problem was only a damp squid. McNamara and Guinan prevailed. That's Roger McNamara. They finished it in two months, just in time for Roger to head back to Ireland and the girlfriend, Majella. By the way with a bundle of money. PS. He earned every penny of it. He worked his ass off.

The Republic Bank is done and dusted except for the punch line. The inspector from the Contractors Office will go through it with a fine tooth comb, and we will get a detailed list of items that have to be corrected. The punch list is common practice in every job. Usually somebody from the shop that's handy in patching does that and until that is completed by us, we will not get the final payment. Believe me we will pay particular attention to that, because we are owed a considerable sum of money. Some people think because you are a boss that you don't work, let me tell you from experience, you go home, you're a worker, you haven't a care in the world as far as the job is concerned, when I go home now as a boss, my day is about half done. On the phone to about twenty different people, suppliers of material for the shop and the different building sites. I could go on and on. People looking for jobs, others were complaining about their fellow workers, not doing their end of the job. I very often get to bed at midnight. Most workers don't know that or couldn't care less. I don't blame them for that, they are not paid to worry, but P.S there are a few workers that understand the trials and tribulations of being a boss, but they also know there is a monitory reward if things go well, the way they were intended too. Life goes on regardless, and you can't expect someone else to do the worrying for you. My ultimate goal is not to stay in this business one more day that I have to, by that I mean, we won't be taking on any more jobs, as we have work to take us another five or six years. Twenty years is the most I intended to continue in business, and as we are now close to fifteen years doing this, we really can't take any more contracts until we see a clear picture of where we're at. A few weeks on, the punch list finished and approved at the Republic National Bank and we look forward to getting paid. So the curtain comes down on another job, but not without some troublesome times, with the hired hands, left a few scars, and a couple of wounded protagonists. But even those found a safe haven later on. I got them jobs with somebody else, even better than ours. So that chapter is closed, as we move onto bigger and better adventures, and more importantly the wounds are healed. Lessons learnt for all those concerned.

Back to New Jersey, I haven't been there for a few weeks, but I know the progress, I've been in touch. It's going well, at a good average of panels being installed every day. Its a few months to go yet, but no complaints. The original screw up has now been forgotten, tranquility is the mood now. Thank God.

I forgave the guy for his shortcomings. You see I may not be a good catholic, but I like to think I'm a fairly good Christian.

Connecticut is just a few months away, we are doing several jobs in the city of New York, small ones, two and four men jobs. They fill in the time between the big ones and are just for the loot has to keep coming in to pay the workers, and everybody else that is owed money. I keep thinking of what Pat Larkin said on his way in from the airport, just arrived, he said " Money fucking Melts, what am I going to use for two weeks", but believe me, he was in pretty good hands. He didn't have a worry in the world.

Christmas is around the corner, and Mona and I are planning to go for our first visit in twenty five years to Ireland for Christmas time. To be painfully honest we were a bit disappointed. You see we got used to all the Hoopla and fanfare in the States, all the City lights and all the modern innovations. You know you can't compare the biggest city in the world with a country village in Ireland, our expectations were unrealistic.

But it goes without saying, we did enjoy being with family and friends. The same family and friends we still have when we go back there, and those very same people will not be surprised to hear, Caroline and Martin are announcing their engagement. Not a surprise to the friends and relatives and the people that know them, and we wish them all the luck in the world. A few months away, Mona is already planning for the event. She said, "I'll make them sit up and take notice". Like Frank Sinatra, she will , "Do it My Way". The place will be The Bloomfield Hotel, Mullingar. The owner, I happen to know very well, Ned Reilly. He visited us here in New York; coincidentally he has a marble factory in Mullingar town and a really modern one. He is a lovely man, we had great old chats and of course some of them about the marble industry. He was quick to add, that he wouldn't be doing big commercial jobs that we do, but he was doing a very big business with Fireplaces, Bathroom Vanity tops, and floor tiles in some of the new hotels. He brought us out to see his private house, just off the eighteenth green in Mullingar Golf Club. The whole works, downstairs gym, really state of the art, pool tables, handball court. The full Monte, piece de resistance, a twenty foot long bar, as well stacked as the Greville Arms, No Kidding. The Celtic Tiger roaring, like he was alive. I told him about my daughter's upcoming wedding, so he said, "I'll meet you and your wife here on Monday evening. We will have dinner, and with the Manager we will go through what you want on your daughter's big day. You need not have any worries; everything will be taken care of, including the Open Bar for one hour". So all is set for the Big Day. So we drove home, went by Rhode, had a lovely chat with Pat Mulvin, R.I.P, and a couple of drinks to cap off a lovely evening. Pat Mulvin that is, another day in the life of Mona and Denny. While I'm talking about Caroline, I have to tell you about a unfortunate accident that Caroline was in. I was here in the States, of course, I flew back as quick as I could book a flight, went straight from the airport to Mullingar Hospital, I knew in my heart, this was not going to be easy, I'm terribly stressed and agitated, but I am a grown man and will have to face up to it, there are literally no options here, get to the hospital. Information Desk, Caroline McNamara, My Daughter, Could you give me Directions. A nice nurse took me to Caroline. Of course I did not know what to expect. I was walking by her bed hoping that the person I was looking for wasn't her. But that person, said clearly, "Dad". That's all I needed to put me over the top. Took me a few minutes to get my composure, and Caroline started talking. I said keep talking, then she broke down, and she explained everything to me about the accident in detail. It was at a intersection. She thought she was putting her foot on the brake, but it was the accelerator, went straight into a high bank in front of her. Her face cut very badly, bled profusely. Her girlfriend, Maureen Greal, ran to the nearest house for help, there was total confusion, and she had lost a lot of blood. Eventually neighbors arrived with all kinds of towels and tape and bandages, and they stopped the bleeding. The next thing, an ambulance arrived, and whisked her to the emergency in Mullingar Hospital, and the rest is history, and I am delighted to tell you she hasn't a mark or blemish on her face. That was my biggest worry and Mona's is that she would be disfigured. Thank God for a complete recovery and she is all set for Big Day. I spent a couple of weeks with her back and forth to Mullingar, before I went back to the States. The wedding is about five months away. She is out of the hospital tomorrow and will be in care of the best in that field. I'll be giving Mona all the news, I'm glad she wasn't here for the nerve racking moments. Like it or not I have to get back on the job again. I won't be aggressive now for a while, but something comes usually to brighten the horizon, and lift ones spirits and I know that will be Caroline's wedding.

I am going to the Marriott right now, it's in full swing inside and outside, it keeps my mind occupied. Progress is satisfactory, the contractors are good people, the payments are always on time, they like the progress also, because they have to get paid too, otherwise we wouldn't get paid. So we are all happy. Let's surge ahead.

A look into New Jersey. Steady progress. Always hard to get the requisition money from this guy, he's always trying to cut you down if your figures show you need $75,000, he would try and make you take less. But I always insist, we get what we billed for, or the work stops. That has worked (up to now) anyway. There is not a lot I like about this job except it is progressing and that is a positive. We will be starting the job in Hartford Connecticut in a couple of weeks. That's a bit of a challenge. We will get away with Chain Blocks there for hoisting the panels; it's a five storey building. Shouldn't be anything complicated. You have to look at the bright side; we try not being negative about any of our projects, big or small. Right now the small jobs are shoveling cash into the business, every little helps. The wheels of fortune keep turning, one never knows from one day to the next what will happen. But one thing I will guarantee you, there will always be some problem. One guy, a worker came to me as soon as I got to the Marriott, "you forgot to put my vacation pay in the envelope", and I think it was all of twelve dollars. Small stuff, but like I said there will always be something to chew on.

Caroline's big day is almost here and of course it's Martin's big days also. Poor guy, joining up with a tough lot. But we will leave that until we are making the speeches at the wedding.

We have just started the job in Hartford, a couple of days to lay it out, and we will be on our way. It's a bit of a journey for us, but we are using some locals. Four of them and two of our own. Its always a good policy to hire local workers. It creates a good impression. The local business agent recommended those four guys, he said, they were excellent workers. Its peace of mind for us also. I will be back to Hartford, after Caroline and Martin's wedding. They have decided to get married in Ballinabrackey Church. She was running a bit late, so I had to put down the boot, so much so, that when I came to a four way cross roads, I went the wrong one. Caroline was panicking. The road I took was so narrow I could not turn, and to make doubly sure I could not turn, there was a great big tractor and trailer. We should be in the church in ten minutes. Panic is gone, Hysteria has taken over. Suddenly a gateway appears, just what I was hoping for, I pulled into the gateway and you would never believe this, your man in the tractor pulled in after us, that's where he was going. He lived in there. I jumped out and said, "Please back out and drive up the road a little bit". "Ok Denny", he said. We knew each other, a son of Mattie Connors; he backed out and wished us the best of luck. By which time we should be in the Church, but had still fifteen minutes to go. Talk about rubber hitting the road. I actually drove recklessly, but with God's help we got there in twelve minutes actually. Somebody told me just to calm me down, I think, the Bride is usually a few minutes late. It's a traditional thing. That really calmed me down and nobody was complaining. I said Halleluiah, the timing happened to be perfect. The music started, the usual, "Here comes the Bride", and me as proud as a Peacock, kissed Caroline for the last time as a McNamara. When I kiss her again, she will be Caroline Murphy. Thanked Martin and said "She is all yours Martin, take good care of her; I know that goes without saying". It was a lovely ceremony, married by the Rev.P.J.McEvoy, he who has stood the test of time and is still a good friend of the family. He does show up once in a while without calling on the phone, a No, No, but he gets away with it. The usual meeting of friends, good wishes, greeting outside the Church, and little by little everybody disappears, and are now headed for the Bloomfield Hotel, Mullingar, as the open bar will start promptly at three o'clock, in the afternoon, of course. The Reception itself will be done American style, after the Holy Hour, the open bar is closed. The people will take their allocated tables, and of course the pews will be occupied in the traditional manor, strictly staying with all the old customs. All tables will be laid out around the area provided for dancing, Mona engineered this arrangement, to copy the American way of doing the reception, and to give the management great credit, they carried it out to the letter of perfection. Thanks to Mandy O'Reilly, who was a most gracious and charming hostess. The music strikes up and Mona and I are very happy the way the whole affair is off to a lovely start. Martin and Caroline are out on the floor, cutting danock out of it. The crowd is a little shy about getting out dancing but in a few minutes, they will all be out strutting their stuff! A few drinks and they will lose their inhibitions, and sure enough they are all out swinging away. But myself, I was getting a little nervous, took a couple of swigs of the Jameson Whiskey and I'm away. I knew I would be nervous, so I did the cute thing; I had a prompter planted right behind me very close, sitting on a chair. Everybody thought he was a reporter taking down my speech, what they didn't know was that he was telling me sometimes what to say. The speech was written out, and he contributed some of it. But the following is all my own, about the two clans, McNamara's and Murphy's.

My Daughter Caroline and Myself on her Wedding Day

The Gaelic for McNamara is Mac Con Muir, or Hound of the Sea (Sea Pirates). The Gaelic for Murphy is O Muir a Cu, or Sea Pirates, so you can see in the ninth or tenth century, all those pirates or clans fought each other and so logically speaking, those two clans fought each other and its also logical to say that the Murphy's kicked the lard out of the McNamara's. Why! Well if you look in a modern day phonebook, there are five Murphy's for one McNamara, so thats proof, they gave us a hiding. But we don't hold grudges. We have long since forgiven the Murphy's, especially when Caroline is getting a good family to take her, we will bend the rules anytime. So I take this golden opportunity of welcoming Martin into the McNamara Family.

I don't want to bore you anymore about the speeches. Let's get on with the rest of the evening. Everybody is really motoring now, its turning out to be a memorable occasion, and I am over the moon for everybody, especially Martin and Caroline, they are very happy. The wonderful day is drawing to a close; everybody is full of good wishes and apparently are delighted to have been a part of this whole day, and how magnificent and original the celebrations were. They all said it was the most delightful, and unique wedding they ever attended, from beginning right down to the last dance.

The after-bar got everybody in a good mood. Again our sincere thanks to the O'Reilly family, particularly Mandy, the very pretty and very efficient hostess. As the curtain draws and we all relax and start heading homeward in a lot of different directions, quite a few, including the Bride and Groom and ourselves will be staying the night here at the Bloomfield.

Up early this morning, everybody is surprisingly chipper at breakfast, despite a rather late night, and no scarcity of the good stuff. Breakfast finished and everybody is headed for home. That is except the Honeymooners. They are heading to Spain for a couple of weeks. Might as well. They will have plenty of time to get back into the harness, and start working. Right now work isn't even in the back of our heads. Hugs and Kisses and best wishes for an enjoyable Honeymoon, as they exit the Bloomfield to cheering and clapping. They shouted, "We will see you all in a couple of weeks".

The next day Mona and I are headed back to the States, to face the music, except I am not expecting to hear music; complaints would be more like it. I'm trying to figure out where I will head for first, so I decided it would be Hartford.

Beautiful fine day, I will see what this recommended crew are all about. It laid out simple enough and no problems were anticipated, and Thank God I was happy to see quite a decent lot of installation done. I sent one of the lads for coffee and sandwiches, as it was lunch time anyway. I told them I was happy with the progress, and they were grateful for those compliments. They really made my day. We checked all the remaining panels and setting materials, and the comment I am making is, those guys are good, and know what they are doing. I did a little quick math myself, and we will be making out well to very well on this one. I told the lads, if they continue this kind of progress, we will give them a nice little bonus. I'll tell you they were delighted. The Foreman jumped up and said to the rest of the men, "Let's go, get that Bonus". I have always said, if you remember, you get more with honey than you do with vinegar. I'm on my way home, tired, after all the goings on, and looking forward to a nice dinner with Mona and also a good night's sleep. That certainly wouldn't hurt. Taking a peek into the Marriott at first sight, I can see some progress made, but I am not sure yet if it's enough, until I see how much we have spent on it. I'm doing the square footage from the drawings. I'll take a look at the balance sheet of the job. Twelve thousand square feet, et at $40 a square foot, a lot of it is granite, don't forget. We've spent about 65-70 thousand, about four and a quarter – it's just on track, we will just have to rev up a little bit. I'm going to spend a couple of weeks now to get this moving a little, we don't want to let it go any slower. "We'll rev it up, John for a few weeks", I said. "I thought it was going alright", said Big John. "Not really", I said, "I'll be back here on Monday, and we will see if we can do something about it". The derrick men came up with a new problem. "We are not allowed by Union rules to take the money from Big John, his trade is ornamental Iron worker", they said. "John will pay you, I'll be giving all the pay envelopes to John and he is my supervisor on the job, not an Iron Worker, he resigned from that Union", I told them. These guys were so tough. At first they thought they were, but no doubt they would rise a row in a empty room. That ended that bullshit. I said to one of them, "if you don't take your pay, I'll leave it into your Union office". "No, No, we'll take it", they said. Never a dull moment. Now next week I have to devise a plan to get around them. I called their business agent and made an appointment with him. He happened to be a nice man, so I told him about the two men of his on the job. The way they were giving me a hard time. "I'll tell you what I'll do", he said, "I'll give you a man that will work. You take care of him with some extra money in his envelope. He is a nice man, with a big family and they won't bother him, he would take care of six of them at the same time". He showed up Monday morning. He spoke with his two colleagues briefly and then he went to work. They never bothered him; you see they control the supply of panels to the stone masons, just to prolong the job. The job took off and in three weeks, we were back way ahead of schedule. You have often heard it said, and so have I, "you have to be the head and tail of your own business". I hate to bore you with details, but please bear with me, it's the nuts and bolts of my life story.

System working, like Willie Nelson, "we're on the road again". I can go other places in comfort, like play a game of golf with the

Woodlawn Golf Club. Leaving in the morning, for Florida, playing at Rolling Hills, it's a good course, 6,900 yards. They played the US Senior Open Championships there a few years ago, and it was also where CADISHACK was filmed. You remember that movie, it featured, Rodney Dangerfield, Chevy Chase among three or four other well known actors, Well anyway we were there for a week. The entertainment was very good. The food also great and the Craic "mighty". Eddie Crowe won the Big Prize, and the runner up was Paddy Casey. There was only one stroke divided those two, very consistent players. The bar in the beautiful clubhouse was magnificent; it must have been at least seventy five foot wide and elevated seat, two armed, and looking straight down the eighteenth fairway. How about a lovely cocktail in front of you, I don't think Paradise could be any better, and Mike McInerney singing "the old Bog Road" and the waiter announcing dinner will be served in about forty five minutes. That was all fairly well planned and plenty of time to get merry. Nobody but Nobody enjoyed this better than my sister in law, Bridget Wood – nee Coyne, and her man of the world, the one and only Andy Wood, by the way, all the way from the capital of the world, London, England, and some of our very popular and well known pub owners, just to mention a few, Mike Carty – Rose O'Gradys New York 51st and 7th Avenue, Martin Griffin – Jug O Punch Jerome Avenue Bronx, Paddy Casey – Casey and Byrnes Bronx 231 St, Bailey Avenue, and I myself have a condominium in the complex here. Flying back this evening after a really enjoyable golf outing, the lads liked so well we actually booked the same week for next year again, that's how much we liked the whole set up here at Rolling Hills Golf and Country Club because I happened to have a condo here, I recommended this place to the Woodlawn Golf Club, and they were all delighted with the place. Tony Brady is another publican that played with us. His pub is Rosie O Grady's, Down Town

Manhattan others who really deserve to be mentioned are the O 'Meara brothers, Phil and Tommy. Great club members and rarely ever misses a tournament. Another loyal clubman Pat Costigan and a tough competitor low handicap Owen Kearns, if Owen was up for the game, he could beat any of us long hitters. Syl Nugent the longest hitter in the club, not forgetting Mike Donavan and Pat Cowan, Syl was always, well nearly always putting for eagles on the par fives. The Rat Pack was D McNamara, Cowan and Donavan, I'll never forget we were on our way home from a golf tournament in Hill and Dale golf club and down about five miles there was a big cook out going in full swing, it was a big green area, they had big barbeque cookers, with big steaks leppin' on them. We just came out of the far side door and joined the line. Some people said to us, "You don't look familiar", "no" I said. We knew one of the principles here; I took a shot in the dark at a name. "We knew John very well, in fact he is a friend of the family", "Is that John Mc Stay" "That's right". "Oh no problem if your friends of John's, carry on". We get one of those big platters, there were two sizes, and we were starving. There must have been two sixteen ounce steaks and big cobs of corn, some lovely roasties. The platters full to the brim, we were looking around guilty as hell. We shuffled our way into the bar, way back in the rear of the bar, it was beautiful, a table to ourselves, it's too good to last, we agreed. I sent Cowan up for three pints; we never enjoyed a meal in our lives as good as we were starving. As we were about to leave this man said to me "John Mc Stay, here, could I speak to you for a minute". "Yes" I said, "I'm on my way to the toilet, I'll be right back" "Take your time, no problem" He replied. I first peeked out the toilet door and as luck would have it he was facing the other direction, Cowan and Donovan they made a run for it and me after them into the car and down the Saw Mill River Parkway, and we laughed the whole way home. P.s, only we had a few drinks in us, we would have never had the courage to try that, drink can give you false courage. That was the end of a day never to be forgotten. Normally we would never do something like that. I better get back to my job again. I hope I'm not boring you with the details of the job but they are really a part of the life story. I hope to lighten up as I go forward with the rest of the story, I promise you there will be fewer details, I said before, Hartford going ok with no problems, this could turn out to be a successful venture, fingers crossed. Another year has passed and Roger is coming out for the last time for his usual three or four months. He is finished in Dominican College in Newbridge. He did an extra year. He's nineteen years old now, he will be back in the Marriot, This time he will be doing bathrooms, remember, we have seven hundred and fifty of them to do, walls, floors, vanity tops and sinks, we will do one bathroom with him and he will take it from there. It's easy teaching him as he's been involved in almost every aspect of the marble business. Down stairs to the derrick men and Big John peace has broken out, the war is over and they are all talking to one another, Hallelujah. Big John has just swallowed six Hamburgers for lunch with four orders of French Fries and a liter of diet coke. Not bad, you say, yes it was bad, I had to pay for it, twenty dollars for lunch, no problem to Big John, and after all he only weighs three hundred and eighty pounds, its only twenty seven stone and two pounds. He was in a restaurant in Dallas, Texas one time and it said on the cover of the menu anybody who can eat a thirty-two ounce steak can have it for free. Believe it or not Big John downed it. Imagine two pounds of steak; it would be enough for four people. Nobody would be surprised if the toilet backed up. That's why he is called Big John. This little episode is interesting, I don't go back to the factory too often, but It was a good thing, I did, Johnny Kapaske, who is the foreman and by and large he's able to keep a lid on things, so he said, "Denis, I want to talk to you, the boys are here after starting something that has never been done here.", So I said, "What's that". They came up with this idea about polishing the edges of the marble. "What's the idea", I said. "Well", he said, "They figure they could polish the edges sitting down on stools". "Where are the stools to begin with", I said, "They figure you will buy them stools". "Yes", I said, "I will buy them stools, but for one reason only, so as they can sit at home looking out the window, waiting for another job. So talk it over, among yourselves". Johnny said, "Your Roger's father. I think he might be the ring leader, go over there and kick him in the butt, and that will bring him to his senses". I had to laugh, if it was Johnny's son, he would definitely kick him in the ass, so I said to them, "You want me to bring in a new crew here?" They all said in unison, "No", "Well stand up polishing the edges, you see Howie would be soft with them and give in. But its traditional to do the edge while standing, it's impossible to polish sitting down, a nice lazy way, but it wouldn't work, end of story. A storm in a tea cup.

Now I will begin a chapter that's a real scandal. For a few years now this individual, who is the culprit, was the leading light in our company. We taught him to do everything in the shop, showed him how to operate all the machines, and he became very good doing anything and everything. He could drive the Hi Lows, the Lo Los, The Trucks, The station wagons, The Whole Bit, even deliver material into the jobs in the City, and New York wasn't easy to get around. I know I've been there and back. He was very good on the big cutting machine, on it was a thirty six inch diamond tipped blade, twelve foot table, the biggest in the business. He was doing this for five or six years now. He knew everybody, I will go back later, to all the other things he was doing, but let me tell you first what done him in. You have heard the word GREED, absolutely hungry for money, he didn't care if it was the middle of the night he had a client. He would think nothing or doing it, and show up for work in time. Just to make it a little more dramatic, I'm holding back with what nailed him. You see he was getting to the point, that he was doing fairly big jobs, while still carrying out his daily routines in the shop, I only found it out much later, that half of the cutting he did in the shop was for himself, and God knows who else. You could never keep this quiet on your own, you would have to have more than one accomplice, but let me tell you something else devious about this character, he had a side job on a Sunday, bar tending in Gaelic Park, the home and head quarters of Gaelic football in the States. It was actually 238st in the Bronx, New York. He was teamed up with a friend of mine. I just could not believe what they were doing. I never sat at the end of the bar that those two worked, not that I had anything against it, but I liked this cozy nook where I sat. A Kerry man was the barman there. I just can't remember his name. He told me they had a five gallon pail, under the counter, that was for putting the tips into. The system was this; after a couple of hours drinking, some of the lads would start to nod off, I don't know, certainly some readers of this have not been to New York, you put your money on the counter and the barman takes the price of the drink or drinks. They are, as a general rule, very honest, most guys would put a twenty spot on the counter. Now in the Gaelic Park scene, the rules were a little different, some of those young lads out from Ireland and also a few not so young, start dozing off. That's when the five gallon pail sprang into action. The squeegee was great to getting the counter clean and dry; the dollars just got in the way and found themselves in the five gallon pail. I saw with my own two eyes, young lads, waking up and asking those two barmen, "I had money here in front of me, what the fuck happened it". "We know nothing about it, are you accusing us of stealing your money?", of course the young men knew better, but in other cases where they were brave and made the mistake of saying, "you must have taken my money", they would be taken out by a couple of thugs and beaten up. This Kerry man told me and explained the whole scenario to me, a great place not to be, as the old mafia guy said, and "include me out". So you see the kind of shady character, I thought was a half God almighty turned out to be the wolf in sheep's clothing. A conservative estimate on the tips for a Sunday would be four hundred, divided between the two of them, plus $100 wages, not a bad days pay, $300 each.

Now the real story begins on my worker crook, with balls bigger than any Jackass, and nerves of steel spelled "Steal". It begins like this. It so happened I had a date with a friend to play a game of golf this evening, in a lovely par three golf course, in Rockland County, the most picturesque layout you ever saw. Little did I think that this little social outing on my favorite golf course would turn out to be the kernel of bad news? It turned me skeptical of, and about everybody in the shop and their friends working for us on the outside jobs. All of a sudden, my American dream was starting to fade, in fact I was thinking out loud. How come my partner could possibly not have seen what was going on? My logic tells me, he would have to ignore what was going on. Why would he ignore what was going on? Case Closed, "Money" (The real, real story) My friend and I teed off, we were chatting away, electric buggy, too hilly to walk. So he said, "You are doing a job in South Jersey, I see". "What do you mean, you see," I said. " Well I was down in South Jersey last night to a friend's house for dinner, and I met a truck with a big load of marble on it, a lot of panels, a swinging load, Your company name on it". "Did you know the driver", I asked. "Yes, stopped at a light…." he told me the driver's name, I used an expletive that I couldn't put on paper. So he said, "Has Denis got a job down here? he said Yes, that was all, the light went green and he sped off". So I said to my friend, "thank you for the information, I can't finish this game". I didn't hit any more balls, but I let my friend finish out the round. He really thanked me for letting him finish out the round, as he needed the practice. He was playing in a tournament at the weekend and he added "I know how you must feel". I am not sure that anybody would know that, but I have to face the music. Monday morning arrived; I went to the usual place to see if any of the Bronx crew wanted a lift down to the shop. There were four of them, they got into the station wagon, three of them in the back seat, and Judas, had the utter gall to get into the front seat. They were probably all in this thing together, but I don't know that yet anyway. I said to Judas, "I hear your doing a job in South Jersey", he was brazening it out to the end. "Neil", I said and he, Neil, spoke to you when you were stopped at a light, he knew who you were the minute he saw the marble company name on the truck, he actually had the nerve to say, that dirty rat. I said to him as soon as you get down to the shop get all of your junk together and leave the building immediately and king balls said "what about my redundancy?". "I'll give you ten minutes to get out and if you don't I'll call the immigration department and you'll be deported in twenty-four hours, don't try to get money from my partner because, I figure for that one job alone, and now I'm hearing there were more, you owe us at least forty thousand dollars. When he heard all this, and that was just what I know now, there were others for sure, he was out of here like a flash. He knew the game was up and that I meant business. This whole upheaval sent suspicious bells ringing in my ears. The only one in the office and shop and yard that I knew had no act or part in all of this was a true and trusted employee, John Kapaska and he hadn't the slightest idea about the stealing that was going on. He would not be a part of anything devious. This day I won't forget, it took a lot out of me and I'm glad it's over. Home for a couple of cocktails with Mona and to rehash the going's on. This day has changed my whole plans for the future, my goal now will be planning not to continue in this business but gradually phase out by finishing the jobs we already have and not take on any more new ones. We still have about three years work. I have quite a few friends, both here and in Ireland and I don't plan to end my days as a couch potato, not by a long shot, I have the old game of golf and intend to hack at that once or twice a week. My mind is set out of this business, in a timely and orderly fashion leaving all that behind for now; I'll get back to the current progress of the jobs. I feel better already after getting rid of that crook. We will play it by ear for now and listen for answers that might be blowing in the wind.

The Marriot is doing fine. That one big tough Derrick man, made a huge difference. The pressure is off Big John, he can have his six hamburgers and three sides of French fries in comfort but, of course not without problems like most jobs, this one has a very fancy entrance big arch. The steel structure that carries, more than a thousand pieces, is a masterpiece in itself. So we have to have our most skilled stone setters on this, with a marble setter to ensure every piece is set in place properly and that will be a man named Jimmy Guinan all the way from Crinkle near Birr in County Offaly. He has a good head on his shoulders for this precise standard of expertise. Jimmy's the man back on the inside, the bathrooms are going at a steady place and we will be ready for the deadline. Roger is putting the finishing touches on the Rotunda. A couple of weeks will get him there, as he will be on his way back to school in Dublin and back to the girlfriend, so we won't be seeing him for a while. I'm not forgetting the job your man 'the crook' started in South Jersey, it's not nearly finished. The owner told me he gave over a five thousand deposit for the work that was done, the owner also told me that he said everything was above board, that he consulted with the bosses, all of which was not true, I absolutely knew nothing about it, my partner Howie, he knew nothing about it. I can't understand how that could be, and he right there in the shop. There were twenty-five panels on the truck the night Mr. X was caught red handed, so they have to be set, so as we can take measurements for the remainder of the job, I made a deal with the owner so much per square foot for whatever it takes to finish it. He signed an agreement to that effect and that will be the end of that chapter of greed. I don't ever want to see that face, again, unless on the obituary column.

I have had great fun with the Woodlawn Golf Club over the years and I have many great memories, some of my best friends were also members of the club, we had a lot of great outings and I might add very competitive. The best golf was played on the nineteenth hole. Also, we had one guy who was the best wood player in the club and was always noted for his consistency, the best wood in the bag was the Pencil, hard to beat that wood.

Roger is back in Ireland telling the girlfriend the good year he had and will be attending a business college in College Green, where I believe it is located. Caroline is settled into their new home in Edenderry and enjoying life in the early stages of their marriage. She actually started to work in Tullamore Hospital as a nurse; she is a fully qualified R.N. It's a nice handy little number for her, half hour each way. She was telling me about the slippery roads over there in the winter time, treacherous. Mona is planning a few days in Spain with Caroline and Martin and some of the kid's maybe; it's nice there in summer time. Somebody told me the cost of living there is less than in Ireland, eating out is considerably cheaper, Mona and I used to go to Majorca, Mona's sister lived there and they had a nice house. What was different about the houses was you parked your car on the street level and walked down the stairs to the floors below and down to the kitchen; everything in the house was either marble or terrazzo. You entered on the top, first like some of my workers would like to do instead of working their way up. Back to the business and Hartford still doing nicely, no problems, that's always good news to hear, I brought those guys to lunch, a great restaurant, all walks of life go in there all construction workers, bankers, school teachers, you name them, there all welcome in that restaurant and everyone is happy. When the guys are doing well its good business to reciprocate, it makes them feel good and you will feel better. Let me break away from that monotonous everyday routine. Well to those out there who have not been on a cruise, try and go on one cruise in your life time, you most definitely will enjoy the ambiance. You will be living like a king; at least for the time spent on the cruise, there is absolutely everything on a cruise, state of art gymnasiums, gambling casinos, gourmet restaurants, and massage parlors. I could go on and on, I never thought a cruise could be so wonderful, the most enjoyable cruise I was on was the last one, my son and daughter treated Mona and I to that one, there were thirteen of us, the grandchildren, Lauren, Evan, Karl, Killian and Tarin, Roger and Majella, Caroline and Martin. Andy and Bridget Wood, Mona and myself. The entertainment on the ship was super, they hire a lot of top class entertainers, there is such a choice of everything, the most of our group generally wound up in the gambling casino, Mona hit for five hundred dollars on the slot machines one night, I didn't do much on the slots but I did spend a good bit of time in this lovely Irish pub. It was located on a street, like a street in any Irish town, those ships are so huge, and that you could spend quite a while looking for your room at night, especially the first night after having a few pints, as good a pint as you would get in any pub in Ireland. The Jameson wasn't bad either, some of the gang came and got me, they knew where to look. They had, among many other sporting facilities, a lovely ice skating rink. The majority of people that used the rink couldn't keep from falling, a lot of first timers on ice but there was one young boy out on the rink and he was like a whiz kid, in and out, up and down at great speed, everybody was looking at him, he was about ten years old and when he was leaving the ice rink, obviously tired, he got a great ovation, he was none other than our own grandson Killian McNamara, I'm sure he felt proud of himself, we certainly did. These are some of the little memories you take home with you, it seven years now since that cruise and Killian is looking at seventeen years old and he is now a quite accomplished ice hockey player, and is a very popular player with Boca Raton High School team and incidentally, his dad, Roger is the coach of that High School team and is also very popular with the team, a big change from working for me on his summer vacation from Ireland. This is just another phase of my life story so hang in there and you will eventually hear the whole story.

Back again to the rather boring monotony of our jobs in progress, the job you remember in New Jersey is nearest to be finished so we will do that one, two or three weeks should wind that one up. We were even from the beginning having difficulty getting performance payments; I'm starting to get bad vibes from this one. This is one of my partners old customers and we won't really give up on trying to get payment before we finish the job, if we have to stop it to get a substantial payment I'll do that, the job went well after a terrible start as you may remember, when the setter cut all the pieces and we had to put them all back together again, remember now? I'm going to his office to get that payment or the job comes to a halt. We will see. It's now tomorrow. Me and my partner are in the contractors office, my partner is a weakling I knew that before we went there at least he is here with me, the meeting starts, the contractor yells at me, "are you trying to rise trouble McNamara". "Yes" I said, "If you don't give us payment that brings us up to date, nothing more will be done on the job until we get that payment". So he turned to my partner and said "is that right Howie", my partner answered "so Dennis says" and the contractor said "What do you say Howie" and Howie said "I have to go along with my partner" the contractor said "You F-----g turn coat!". I immediately knew there was something going on with the contractor and my partner so I said "I'm leaving and if we don't get what I requested, not another panel will be set on that job". Fifty thousand dollars is what he owes us to bring us up to date, I drove straight to the job and explained to the guys what was going on, they went along with the plans, this was Wednesday evening, I told them "I'll pay you, tomorrow which is Thursday and Friday stay at home, enjoy the weekend. If this is not settled by the weekend, I will have a place for you to go on Monday, OK?" It will be interesting to see what the contractor does, and I will get back to my story on Monday, Roger and Caroline are in Ireland, and Mona and I are headed to the Catskill Mountains. That's the Irish Catskills. The weather is very hot, good to get away from the City, nice and cool at night in the mountains. We stay in Pat Moroney's place, a Clare man himself. It's a nice break to getaway for the weekend, away from the battles of Construction. Lovely man Pat gets to say hallo to everyone of his guests. Plenty of good wholesome food and most importantly, a fine lounge and bar. It's a great get away for the Irish. All the motels, hotels, restaurants, and golf courses are owned by the Irish from Ireland, or Irish Americans. But I have to face the music Monday morning.

That old Monday morning feeling is here as I head down to the shop and confront my partner, to see what happened in the meantime. So he told me, the contractor went ape-shit, about the balls I had to stop his job, and I said, "Good, I'm glad he did, that donkey from Ireland he's got some Callooas (name for balls)". He said, "If the men are back there this Monday morning, you can pick up 50,000 Wednesday". So I got on the phone and told the guys to go right back to the job this morning and keeps it going like you have been doing. Talked to the guys in the shop, as I haven't seen them in a good while and my old friend Johnny

Capaski and I went down to the Marriott to see what was happening there. Some nice lolly coming from there at a steady pace. I'm happy enough with this job. Home now for dinner with Mona and chat about the lovely weekend at the Catskills, a couple of cocktails and we are ready for a good night's rest. The pressure is always there, we are down to seventy five guys but it's a big nut to crack, God's good and so is Bill Burke. On St.Patricks day I get invited upstairs. A beautiful view of the Parade passing by, on glorious Fifth Avenue. St.Patrick's magnificent Cathedral where Mona and I got married, right across the street, a nostalgic atmosphere, buoyed by a couple of nice fancy glasses of Bailey's Irish Cream and your looking close to the edge of utopia. Bring it on ladies and gentlemen; good times don't last long enough. Business had to be taken care of. Down for the check on Wednesday. He handed me the check, $50,000, O.K certified, O.K an official company, Date stamp on it. "Hold it", I said, the date stamp on the check was postdated. "So that means one thing," I said, as I got my phone, "I'm stopping the men on the job". He whipped the check from my hand and uttered something inaudible. Probably, "you donkey bastard", or something worse maybe. He wrote out another check, got it certified with the proper date. I went straight to the Bank of Ireland with it. They put it through the system, and it was OK. At that minute I was thinking to myself – will this be the last money we will get from this low-down creep. I wish I could fast forward this job and see what we will be doing when it's completed. I will be letting you know later on in the story (True Story). As soon as the check cleared, I put the men back to work. Let me tell you right now, it's not easy. It's the survival of the fittest. I'll be back for the final chapter in this difficult situation. At this time the vibes are not good. Back to Connecticut. This one is like a breath of fresh air. Never a problem. These guys, if I must say so, have a conscious and do a day's work for a fair days pay. That's what makes life easy for both sides of the equation. I'm late for lunch lads, but not purposely. It's about 2:30 in the afternoon. I sent the young guy out for coffee and we sat down and chatted for a while. What a different atmosphere. I paid them, it's time to go, as they are entitled to an hour to change their checks, union rules, and the owner left my check with the foreman, a nice little one, fifty-five G's, not too hard to take coming into the weekend. "I'll be busy, I won't see you next week", I tell the crew. Down to the Marriott to see how they are doing there. It looks like they are going good. Monday we are starting this monstrosity of an arch. The supporting structure is all steel and Big John has got all his measurements marked out with the direction of Little Benny, the draughtsman, who is absolutely brilliant. The other Marble Contractors in the city steered clear of this job because of its entrance arch. The arch, we just laid out, I was in on the lay out myself. As I think I am no back of a clock. So we will be on our way Monday morning. There is one other guy that will be there for sure, The Jimmy Guinan. Because it is an artistic masterpiece, and the Big derrick man, if you remember, straightened out the whole difficult labor situation, I am very happy to have that Big guy Jimmy Guinan and Big John on our side. We need all the inspiration and luck on our side for this one, as the big boys passed this job up. But with a little luck and a lot of big balls, we will pull it off. God willing. I did a little Math on it, and we are right on schedule, up to now that is, but a tough road ahead. The big beautiful arch will take time and expertise, time of course, eats up money. I spoke with the project manager, and he thinks we are falling behind a little bit, and I reminded him that we were actually six weeks behind the time we were originally supposed to start, the job wasn't ready on time, so the blame cannot be put on us. So I suggested that we start working overtime. He said, "Where will the money come from, as we are on a tight budget". I replied, "Not my problem". He replied, between you and me that building really had to open on the scheduled date, as there are a whole month of banquets, conferences and union conferences booked. "Well," I said, "get your act together, as time is of the essence. We have unions involved here, and they are strictly double time for overtime. You alert your men and I will let you know shortly". It didn't take long, The Marriott, a huge hotel chain gave him the go ahead. The lads in the New Jersey job, you know the bum we have trouble collecting from, they might be looking for a piece of the action, we will have to see what we can do. Big John will mastermind something; I have no doubt about that. We have to pull this job out of the fire somehow; but with our expert crew and Big John I'm confident we will do it. The Good Lord might have a little compassion also. This happens to be a holiday weekend. We will start to work overtime on Monday, and it will be helter skelter down to the wire three months from now or four. Meanwhile we will be busy in other places, trying to get the Hartford one finished.

I was at the opening of a New Irish Pub last night. The name they put on it, was BROGUES. You all know what that means. A Meath man is the owner, and another Meath man will be the manager. The owner's name is Pat Kinsella, from Slane. Slane is famous for a few things; Slane Castle for one, and Brian Boru fought a famous battle there, I'm sure you all know the history of that one. Brogue's bar will also have a very spacious restaurant. With tables for four people, six, eight and ten. Also booths for four people, six and eight. It was quite a good menu with American dishes. Also Irish specialties', Corn Beef and Cabbage, Irish Limerick Ham, Roast Duck, fresh Salmon, Red Snapper and Kilappiti, and many other International dishes. I know Pat Kinsella well from the construction business. He is an architect by profession and wouldn't be hurting for a few dollars, or a few brains either. The manager's name was Clem McAuley, a first cousin of the Meath Full-Back, Darren Fay. I met Fay there a couple of times, a very athletic looking dude. I saw him playing Croke Park a few times. For years I didn't miss many games in Croke Park, the semi finals and finals, and sometimes with my old friends, Paddy and his brother Fr.Dan Moore, and of course, the one and only Bernie Dowling. Bernie never missed a match that Meath were playing in. They were the Good Old Days, on our way home from Croke Park, we never missed calling into a pub/restaurant called "The Huntsman", one of the best carveries in the country. You name what you want and they have it at reasonable prices. While having a meal we would make sure we sat opposite a big television, with a beverage of your choice. They also had a great pint of Guinness, that was my choice, and we watched the game all over again. I'll tell you, it doesn't get any better than that. As a matter of fact, you see the game much better, and you know who has the ball all the time. Watching the game in the stadium in Croke Park, I know I have problems knowing who has the ball. The announcer tells you everything, for us this is fantastic. The announcer fills in all of what you missed at the game. I think we'll have another pint lads, don't let on to anybody!

What with drink driving laws, we have to be careful, lucky we have a chauffeur that doesn't drink alcohol. As we head for home, where most people go, at the end of the day, for us a most enjoyable one, as our team won. You will have observed that I am in Ireland now. Heading back to the States at the end of the week and back to the grinding stone once more.

It's a week later now, and I'm down in Manhattan, where the Marriott is, 46st and Broadway. You all have heard of the Bright Lights of Broadway, where money will buy you anything your little heart desires, well, I brought a chap named Paul Byrne for a stroll down Broadway. He was staring in this brightly lit alcove, and it said, "This is a peep show parlor, if you want a peep, put in a quarter in the slot machine". He duly obliged, and a beautiful blonde appeared in the picture, and totally naked. Paul said, "oh my God". He's actually very religious, "Where is Christine (his wife)?" She was looking at other things down the street, "let's get out of here", he said, "Before she comes back". As a matter of fact she was back and watched him during the whole show. Paul said, "I apologize Christine", and she replied, "you needn't apologize, I always knew you were an auld pervert". P.S, we all had a great laugh. But poor Paul will never live it down. Paul and Christine went into a movie, No, No, this was a nice movie, while I went into the job in the Marriott. The arch, you remember is the big deal. It's moving but as to be expected slowly. All other facets of the job are going nicely; our fingers are crossed hoping to meet the deadline. Let's face it; we have to meet it, as there is an opening date set that has to be met, even if we have to work around the clock. I'll be back here on Monday. I told John, we have to do something. We will put all our heads together and get one Big Head, No, just joking. "See you Monday morning John, put your thinking cap on". I said, "See you then", replied John.

Mona and I headed to the Pocono Nose in Pennsylvania, for the weekend. Paddy and Joan Casey, our good friends are also going. We are playing a golf tournament up there. It's a big long course, and I expect to enjoy it, I don't expect to win anything with my handicap, I can't play off a twelve handicap on that course, but I will enjoy it. The entertainment is always top shelf comedians, a few drinks and good food, and good company, what more would you ask for. We go Friday at noon and will be able to get in at least nine holes of golf. Nice dinner and drinks, great entertainment and we are off to a great weekend. Mona's sister Angela and her husband Tony McCarthy are with us. On board also, Mona's mother and our son Roger, so we are off and running for the weekend. Mona's mother loved to be in the thick of everything. She loved an auld gargle RIP. We thought she was enjoying the comedian, but she coined a phrase, that we still use, and it was, "I never knew a word he said". But she was no spoil sport, she laughed when the crowd laughed. She was a legend in her own time. We all miss her very much. The weekend like all enjoyable outings flew by, and where do I find myself, but back at the Marriott Monday morning. Big John and I agreed to have one helper serve two setters, this way we could hire, two more setters, and would expedite matters for sure, as the Marriott were footing the overtime bill. I suggested to the setters, one brass anchor, instead of two, was plenty for all the small pieces in the arch. We should be gaining momentum. I went back a couple of days later, and sure enough it was looking like we would make the deadline rather comfortably. The pressure was off, and I am on my way back home, and rested, feeling the good times of the weekend, Mona had a lovely dinner and some cocktails ready, and in no time flat, we are both in Cuckoo land, and slept like babies. Woke up to a brand new day, fresh and rested. Stopped by New Jersey, that one is coming down to the wire. A couple of weeks and we will be there. Our biggest worry now is to get the money he owes us. So we will see what happens later on. Connecticut is also coming down to the wire; I wish we had a few jobs like that, no problems.

The Marriott is doing nicely now and we will make the deadline, and the money is flowing steadily in from that one. Big John is doing his homework with the overtime and requisitions. Bill Burke is not complaining. He's the pulse of our company at the moment, but we're making life easy for him, by making steady deposits from the jobs. We keep the grain flowing into the mill, and that's the name of this game. My son Roger came out specially to get a piece of the action with the overtime. I'm glad he was able to come, and get some of the gravy. As soon as the Marriott is over and of course the other jobs will also be finished we will take a break. However we have more jobs coming up, when the dust settles on the present ones. We have other things and events to look forward to, like Roger's wedding, which will be very soon after the jobs are finished. I won't unveil the program yet, until we are close to it, meantime we will keep working hard to get the jobs finished, so we can all enjoy the big occasion. Connecticut has just one week now to being completed, and New Jersey about the same. We are now down to three weeks at the Marriott. The Marriott has already sent out invitations to everybody that done contract work at the hotel. That includes all subcontractors, Mona and I got our invitations, on which we can bring two guests. Roger is not staying for that, he will be heading back to Ireland to his sweetheart, Majella; so, Caroline and Martin will be on board, I heard from the assistant Manager, that nothing will be spared that money can buy, so we are looking forward to that night and especially to Martin and Caroline coming. I saw the big banquet room, it's massive, one week to deadline, and we know we will make it. What pressure. What a relief it will be to put the last piece of granite into its place.

Well Hallelujah, we're there. Three cheers for the men that made it possible, and four cheers for Bill Burke, who really made it possible. Thanks again Bill, you were our life line. The last piece is in place and we are finished. Bring on the banquet, we're ready. Well Caroline and Martin have arrived, one day ahead of the big night. The four of us will go out locally. Probably Longhorns'. It's good for a nice steak, and they make a great Caesars' Salad. They also make a delicious Manhattan, Vermouth and a good Rye Whiskey, topped with a couple of nice red cherries, great for wetting the appetite. So we're here on Congress Avenue, and Boynton Beach Boulevard, in and seated in Longhorns' for an enjoyable evening, before the big night which is tomorrow night. We won't be boozing it up too much, just a couple of cocktails, and Martinis and I will have a pint of beer to cool us down. A good night's sleep and rest, and we will be all set for the Biggie tomorrow night. The ladies will be laying on a bit of style, a dress rehearsal, and then the big decision on what they will wear. For Martin and me, it's relatively simple, but we're bent now on a good sleep tonight.

Saturday evening, on our way Downtown Manhattan, Marriott Hotel, 46th St and Broadway. We arrive there at 7:30pm; we pick up our table number and are escorted to our table by the head waiter. A lovely spacious table for four, with a beautiful big Orchid as a centre piece. The wine steward comes right over in case we might want to order wine. Martin is the wine connoisseur at our table, he orders a nice red, and also a nice white, Mona and Caroline will sip, Martin the red, and I ordered a Manhattan. I have one or two to begin, usually before dinner. The food for tonight will be Buffet Style. The Buffet tables; there are two seventy five feet by about ten foot wide, so we decided to take a tour of both tables first, a dry run, before we decide on what we're going to eat. The head waiter advised us to do that, because people make the mistake of not looking at all the options, and later see, all the delicious gourmet tit bits, that they would have loved, (throat cutting time). We are starting to get in the mood for a good night. The Manhattans and the wines are kicking in, the band strikes up, and believe or not, the first tune is, I'm sure you have heard it before, "When Irish Eyes are Smiling, All the World seems Bright and Gay", and of course we hit the floor dancing. Not a care in the world on us, away from the huge pressure of trying to finish the job, and enjoy this beautiful opening night of the impressive looking Marriott. The people that actually catered this beautiful presentation of food must have known we were a healthy lot of people, because the dinner platters were quite a bit larger than the normal platter. So our plan, all four of us was unanimous – and to take full advantage of the large platters, we all took different foods, you have guessed right, we all shared with each other. Caroline was the table boss, we elected her to that position. The first thing she said was, "Dad leave down your knife and fork, and take it easy". So my knife and fork is down, and the three of them, milling food into themselves. So I get wise to that fairly quickly. We all agreed it was a lavish display of delicious food, up market, first class. All the guys from the job came by the table, as the night progressed. It was like a reunion of all the sub contactors. A night I will always remember, and to have Mona, Caroline and Martin with me was something very special in my life. We danced the night away. All such functions bring down the curtain at twelve o'clock, as people live in the area, that's the law. Everybody is home at a reasonable hour, and that's good as we happen to be practicing Catholics and go to Church on Sunday and Holy days. That's the way we were brought up. Mona and I are taking a few weeks off, and heading to the old country. We have a big occasion, a celebration, an event happening, Roger's wedding, to Majella Boylan, from Dublin. They are getting married in her local church, and that's nice, by a young local priest, and that's also very nice. They are having their reception in Slane Castle, and that's exiting and different. One of the hottest days of the year, and what was also a little different, they came to the castle from Dublin Airport by Helicopter. We gave them a rousing reception when they landed in the lawn right in front of the door to the castle. We got them on camera coming in on the helicopter; it was all very exciting and lovely. The cameras were flicking left, right and centre. It's nice to be young and this is their big day, and Mona and I intend to enjoy every moment of it. In the reception hall, everybody got a welcoming glass of champagne, before going to their tables. The guests were mostly family from both sides. We had people from London, Florida, New York, is all I can remember, Larry Coyne and his wife, from London Eileen – Terry Coyle and May from the Gold Coast of Florida –

Matty Keegan and Rose Marie, and their daughter from New York. I mentioned those people just because they travelled long journeys, and that is very much appreciated. But of course, all the guests are more than welcome, and we hope they let themselves go, and enjoy the wedding celebration of Roger and Majella in this historical old castle, in the heart of County Meath. I say Cead Mile Failtè to everybody and have a wonderful day. One of our special guests from New York, Leo O'Dowd gave a very nice little speech as only Leo can. He was a close friend of Rogers. The Boylan family and the McNamara family were very well represented. The cocktails were flowing, and the spirits were high. The music suited the mood, as guests mingled and chatted, and reminisced, good company and good times should never end. But this day had a beautiful beginning, when Roger and Majella exchanged vows of, I Do. Off on a mysterious journey that as of now, they are not sure where it might take them, but if it's a little short of paradise, we hope it will be the next best thing. A life full of hope and happiness, and raise their children with good Christian principles, where truth and honesty will always prevail. That's enough of preaching. The young priest who performed the wedding ceremony got us all off to a lovely start to the whole day. He was a very affable young and bright man, said all the right things. We were all floating on air as we headed for the castle, only to see the Helicopter floating right down to the entrance. I must say Mona and I were over the moon, at that particular moment, memories so beautiful. Meeting all our friends, some we haven't seen for quite a while, trying to cram all this nostalgia into a few hours is mind boggling. The loud talk, the laughter, the good wishes, the friendly atmosphere, we never realized we had such nice relatives and good friends. If ever there was a day to remember this would be on the top of the list.

The speech making is about to start. I thanked everybody who intended to say a few words, but if they wouldn't mind to keep it brief, and I'm delighted to say they all did that with the possible exception of me. But that was a given, and I was pardoned. I wanted to thank everybody for making this a wonderful day, and everybody who contributed to make it such a happy and wonderful day. Everybody it seemed was on the floor and they were rocking this old ancient and stately castle. I saw Terry Coyne and Martina Hogan really going at it, they were jitterbugging at a hectic pace. But everything comes to an end and soon this fantastic day, and I'm sure Roger and Majella, with all the tension, will be looking forward to a good night's rest as we draw to a close here. Everybody is saying their goodbyes, and heading back to their homes, except for the Americans, they used this occasion for a few days after the wedding to holiday. We will be in touch before they go back.

Now back again to a very unpleasant situation as soon as I got back to the States, but before that, we have a bit of catching up with some friends and neighbors', our neighbors' in Killane View, The Lowrys, Mary and Therese, The Conlons, Michael and Bernie, Robbie and Sheila and the children, needless to say great neighbors and good friends, and of course Pat Quirke and Tom Crinnegan. We all get along very well. They really are very lovely people. We always look forward to coming back and getting together for a few auld gargles. We usually come back for a few months, departing around October, back to the heat again. We love the summer here, with family, Martin, Caroline and the three siblings, Lauren, Evan and Karl.

A little golf now and again, out at Edenderry Golf Club, Liam looks after me when I play there, I like to have a Golf cart. The old legs are not like they used to be. There are not many courses in Florida better than Edenderry. The lush fairways are definitely not equaled in Florida. The fairways in any course in Ireland are lusher. The climate is the main difference. It's a much damper climate in Ireland. We are planning a game about the first week in July, and we are looking forward to that. The Americans will be in Ireland at that time.

I'm going back now briefly to the job in New Jersey. The one we are having trouble collecting the money we are owed. I don't want to bore you, we have gotten a court order from the State Courts to collect the money, but this contractor ignores everything. What would that tell you, enough said, that this is dangerous territory, and what else can we do. I am suspicious of my friends and I will just say, enough said. One hundred and fifty grand gone down the drain. Take is on the chin and move on. Life is not exactly a bed of Roses. You live and you learn. The best school in the world. The school of hard knocks. A lesson you will never forget, because it hits you in the bread basket. Those people are infiltrating the construction business. But as I think I said earlier in the story, I wasn't exactly happy with some of my own associates. I will also say no more about that for now. Connecticut is now finishing up and good news on that one. It was very good from the very start and never gave me a moment's worry. We need that after the bad one in New Jersey. I am taking these guys out to lunch and a couple of beers, they deserve it. I go home from up here, because it's a bit of a journey fifty miles to where we live in Riverdale, New York. Mona will have the nosh cooking. Mona also has her own business in a place called Kittay House. It's, really for retired people, who happen to be very well off and can afford it. It's really up market, and Mona has the concession thee, a fully equipped beauty salon. Right now I am just looking forward as I drive down the Saw Mill River Parkway on my way home, for an intimate chat and dinner with Mona.

After all the celebrations, life will go on pretty much as usual but we will be talking about them for a while. Now that our son and daughter are married and settling down to make their own way in life, it will also be a big change in our lives. As they assume the responsibilities of hopefully bringing up a family in the traditional way of their background and culture, it will be all so exiting and full of hope for all of us. But thats around the corner and in the lap of the Gods. One never knows in this life what is awaiting them around the corner, time will tell.

Roger and Caroline know we are always here if any problems might surface, but also knowing Majella and Martin, everything will be fine. Those four have plenty of ability to cope with all eventualities. Have no fear the four whizz kids are here.

The jobs around New York are pretty much finished, except for a few smaller ones. They are jobs with about four, five or six workers. The lads are able to handle those jobs themselves, and it leaves us free to move onto something else, and that something else is a job we took on in Boston. I have been up there a few times with Benny, our draughtsman surveying and taking measurements and applying engineer's elevation marks on all the elevations, and walls. Again I don't want to bore you with a lot of details and technical talk. The name of this building now is The General Post Office, No.1 Post Office Square. That will be changed to The Meridian Hotel, and will be the home of the Boston Celtics Basketball Team. There was a time not long ago, when the Celtics ruled the roost in the N.B.A. Let's talk a little about the City of Boston. It's quite a bit like Dublin, Ireland architecturally, almost every cop in Boston, claims some Irish blood in them, or some with all Irish ancestry. So we felt pretty much surrounded by a lot of our own kind, It didn't mean we could go out and wreck the place after we got a few pints, and when you get a few Irish lads together there will be pints. Now we will talk about a few problems we might have when we start installing the marble in the lobby areas. That's exactly where the problems will be. You might say, why that would be a problem. Well from finished floor to ceiling will be seven feet exactly. Somebody said, to let those two seven foot Celtic Basketball players, take of their shoes, and that would solve the problem. But that didn't satisfy the architect, and somehow he was hoping that we would pull some trick out of the hat, so I told him, there is an existing condition here, that we can do nothing about. There is nothing in the specifications about seven foot basket ball players having clear unhindered access to the elevators, as staid and as dour as he was, he smiled. We penetrated his psych and he said, "Is there anything we can do, Mr. McNamara". All of a sudden, I am Mr. "Yes we can do a little," I replied, you could see he was mentally relieved. "What can you do", he said. Well seeing as the floor marble is not ordered yet, instead of one and one quarter inch, we can do fine with three quarters of an inch. We can grind the structural steel to a smoother finish, and we will paint it exactly the same color Beige as the marble, and we have down in our factory in New York a man who will make the steel look exactly like the marble veins and the whole bit." I replied" He was over the moon because he will get the credit for it, at least he thinks so. So he said, "Where are you staying here in Boston". I told him, in a motel a couple of miles out. "Do you know Quincy Market?" he asked. "Yes I do", I replied. He gave me his card with writing on it. "Go to Morahans Steak House and give the waiter this, and have dinner on me". Benny and I went, and being that it was a steak house, we had the best in the house, and a couple of nice cocktails, a most enjoyable evening. But the big victory was to have the architect on your side; we will pick up this part of the story a little later.

Mona and I are taking advantage of a little slow down in our business and will travel to see some of the American countryside. Deep down we are country people, at heart, and intend to enjoy this couple of weeks. Mona has someone to fill in for her, so we are all set. The first stop we decided on was Hartford Connecticut. You remember we just finished a job there. We booked in to a nice motel on the edge of town, nice and convenient to shops and restaurants. We rested a while and freshened up for the shops. Mona happens to love a bit of shopping. After shopping, we drove into the heart of town; Mona took a fast look at the style in the clothing stores, very impressed with the style, but not with the prices. She bought a blouse and skirt. She said they were drop dead gorgeous, and so was the price. We are getting hungry and I know a very nice restaurant not far from our motel, walking distance if we have to. I had my favorite dish of all times, Red Snapper in a bag, out of this world. Mona decided on Surf and Turf, when translated is Lobster tail and Fillet Mignon. We had shrimp salad starters, a couple of nice cocktails to whet the appetites, and we were on our way to a magnificent evening, and even if I do say so I well deserved. We spent three days driving around, mostly western Connecticut and enjoyed every moment of it, then crossed over into New York State. By the way it's the fall, or as we would say autumn and the trees are so beautiful. All the colors of the rainbow. It was evening time as we headed into upstate New York. The sun was on its way down. The rays were shining through the trees. The sun itself was a ball of fire. We got into a parking space because we wanted to get this magnificent panorama as the sun glistened in the settled rivers, racing down the mountain sides. The greatest artists ever known, could not paint the views we were looking at, and with a cooling evening breeze rustling the leaves, was something only the Good Lord could accomplish, added to by nature's orchestra, the birds singing and whistling their merry tunes. New York State in the Fall, is a must to visit and see. We really like and enjoyed New York State, stayed in motels in rural areas, but are now headed for Boston City. I always wanted Mona to see Boston. It would remind us of Dublin quite a bit. The Police forces have a lot of Irish Americans, and some directly from Ireland. But of course there are other nationalities as well. The Pubs and Restaurants are either owned or run by Irish, so you can understand why the Irish like Boston. There is one particular area that is the most popular, its Quincy Market, food, clothing, restaurants, and pubs galore. It's a real live area, and always thronged with people. Mona was impressed and why was she impressed, there were top of the range clothing stores. We are staying three or four days in Boston. She would stay in Quincy Market for those four days, but we had to push on. I showed her the hotel we were doing the marble in. The only interest she had in that was (how much will you make (bread) and bragging rights), typical, purely mercenary. We go back to our hotel freshen up and get ready for a nice meal in Quincy Market with all the travelling we were a little tired, so we rested for a while. OK, rested and ready, a nice meal preceded by a couple of appetizers, to whet the appetite. Our starters were Stone Crab, with the appropriate sauce, main course, Mona had Fillet Mignon, veggies and some roasties. That sounded so good, I had the same, and believe me, and we both laid back our ears. The waiter said it was the first time; he could ever put plates back directly on the shelf. Believe it or not. We spent our third day in Boston, and are on our way back to Riverdale. That's where we live; it's on the Borders of Westchester County. It's really the last bastion of Law and Order, in the North West Bronx. Me and my crew, will be back in Boston next week, in the meantime we got a job in the City of Newark, New Jersey it's a railways station. We are doing the marble on the sides of the escalators. They are really used as hand rails. They are one foot wide and five foot deep, and there are lots of them. Somebody had the job and gave it up, for what reason I don't know. But we agreed to do it, time and material, we billed them every week for our cost plus twenty five percent profit. It was signed and sealed, guaranteed money to be received every Thursday, Union Rules. This is one time, that it's nice to have the Union behind you. We are a Union Shop anyway, this one is really grease for the mill, (How Sweet it Is, Jackie

Gleeson's famous quotation). We will put a steady ten man crew there, and we have a man tailor made for the job. "Big John" and it's also near where he lives. This will suit him down to the ground. He's like the golfer who used to win a lot. He was a great wood player. The best wood in his bag was the Pencil. John is also very good with figures, but this job is cut and dried. The State of New Jersey Railroad Company, now and again, you get lucky. The last job in New Jersey turned out to be a baddie. I told you about that one earlier, we never got the one hundred and fifty thousand dollars we were owed, so we needed this one. Thank God for it.

Now I'm on a whole different set of circumstances. Boston, here we come. This will be a challenge, and to see if we can pull it off, will take our best efforts. To begin with we have to have one local worker, for everyone we take with us, from New York. That should not make a big difference, as the local union representative told me, he will give us the cream of the crop, in other words, you look after me, and I will look after you. "Sounds OK to me," I said. That is a really big headache taken care of; as long as the workers are happy one can expect smooth sailing. I had lunch with the business agent, and he was very happy and will be with us every step of the way. The job will take about twelve months to complete, so we are ready to start this coming Monday. All the marble is on the site, and the first task for the workers is to open all the crates and stack the marble near where it will be installed. Normal procedure. I will go through the blue prints with the two foremen and our draughtsman Benny, and make sure they understand, the drawings which will be no problem to experienced foremen. Benny will be there in a little office we made for him, and will answer any questions the workers might have. Once we get started the tension will subside. When the first slab of marble is in place, and the workers get familiarized I'll be on my way back home. Mona and I have a few things to take care of.

We have a few Condo's rented out, and in hindsight, we would never get involved again. I am saying the following from experience. Tenants, at least the ones we have, don't respect your property, and also think nothing of being behind on their rent, two or three months. Then one tenant called me on the phone and said, "My washing machine is on the blink, so I bought a new one, I'm sending you the bill". By the way this is the one whose three months behind on the rent. Need I tell you, low life's. It's now on the market for sale, and I will have a problem throwing her out. It took six months to get her out. She tried to take the new washing machine with her. Her neighbor, who is also a tenant of ours, a first class gentleman, phoned me, of her intentions, so I told him, "Let me know when she is in the act of taking out the washing machine". I got there with a police man; I had a copy of the check and the receipts showing I paid for it. She was actually trying to convince the cop that she paid for it, until he showed her the receipt and the cancelled check. He gave her a summons and a date to show up in court. The charge was attempted robbery. I heard through the grapevine that she did three months in jail, and it wasn't her first time, and probably won't be the last. P.S, I since sold it, and believe it or not made a profit after spending nine thousand dollars to repair the damage that she caused. That my friends are the downsides of renting and renting in general is no picnic. I have a couple more to get rid of and they will also be good riddance. I am not done yet; myself and Mona hopped on a plane to a town called Clearwater, Florida. A nice looking development. We also had two condos there, and also luckily had one of our all time best friends living in the same complex. Her name, May Scanlon, a lady of the highest order, and her husband, Brendan, a gentleman. Altogether we did four cruises with them. The ships names were, The Michael Angelo, The Leonardo da Vinci, The Queen

Elizabeth the Second (twice), so when I say good friends, you'll understand that we really were. We have the two condos in their complex. Don't get me wrong, one of them was rented by an elderly couple, that's the one that was in bad repair. They were old and they let it get run down. We, with the help of May and Brendan went out and bought the material, that we had carefully made up a list of "to do" repairs. May knew a carpenter who did repair jobs. He gave us a price, and we in turn gave him the job. We stayed with May and Brendan, and went out every night, and had a great old reunion, talked about old times, and the memorable cruises that we enjoyed so much, and the way we missed them so much when they moved to Clearwater. We are with them now, when a knock came on the door. The carpenter came for his money, seven thousand five hundred dollars; we went with him to inspect the job. It was good and we paid him. The other Condo was in the best of shape. So May knew we wanted to put them on the market. She knew a first class Real Estate Agent, four and a half percent with no hidden extras, and we said go ahead and advertize them for us. May knows our phone number and address. The job is right, mission accomplished. Said our goodbyes to great friends, and we are always in touch anyway. Goodbye and God Bless to May and Brendan Scanlon.

The Boston Hotel is going smoothly. It's now three months since it started. The progress is about what we expected, a very reputable contractor, no problem with payments. Karl Murphy is here, and also his mam Caroline. He has played a lot of golf with his two cousins and myself. If he keeps interested in the game, he should be a very good golfer. He had a lot of fun with Killian and Tarin. They got on with each other very well, and already he is looking forward to coming out again soon. The Floridians are coming to Europe for a travelling vacation. They are visiting four or five countries in Europe and of course Ireland for nine or ten days. We will get in some golf in the home course, Edenderry for sure. Our friend Liam, looks after us, and makes sure we have golf buggies and a nice lunch after the game, and a couple of pints. The Yanks are looking forward to it already. That will be late June or early July. I am also looking forward to that myself. I am on my way out to Newark to see what's happening there. I haven't heard any complaints. Big Jon and I have lunch. He is as happy as Larry, whoever Larry was. He was saying that everybody should have one job like this every year.

We are planning a tail-gate party for the big American Football game for our company, and I am going to get John to run it, There are people that do that kind of catering, Big John knows all of them, and he assured us we would get a good deal. They will be all excellently presented, steaks, chicken, sausages, loads of them, and all kinds of bread – Italian rolls, French bread, the whole works, and all the beer you can drink. It's planned to last about one and a half hours. The game starts at eight thirty, so we are telling our workers, and special guests to arrive at approximately six o'clock. This way they have plenty of time to party.

The Odd Couple – P.McCormack (The Iron Man) & Pat Larkin

97th ANNIVERSARY
DINNER DANCE

County Offaly Association of New York, Inc.

"The Faithful County"

The Astorian Manor
25-22 Astoria Blvd. Astoria. N. Y.

Friday, November 22, 1985

To the Best Father

in the whole World

Congratulations and Best Wishes

on being honored by the

County Offaly Association

from

Your Daughter

Caroline Murphy

and Husband

Martin

and Your Son

Roger

County Offaly Association of New York, Inc.

#1

Failte

Cead Mile Failte to the 97th Anniversary Dinner Dance and Reunion of the County Offaly Association of New York, Inc. You honor us by your presence tonight.

We are very proud of the contributions that the sons and daughters of Offaly and their descendents have made to perpetuate Irish Culture, Athletics and Brotherhood throughout the world but especially in the Greater New York Area.

Our Guest of Honor this year, Denis McNamara was born in Ballinabrackey. Since his years as a prominent footballer both in Ireland and New York he has distinguished himself as a successful businessman in New York and has helped many young people get their start in America.

We especially wish to thank all those advertisers who have given their financial support to this journal, we urge all our friends to support these people.

Thus far this year we had a very large turnout at our Annual Memorial Mass and Communion Breakfast in February and a large contingent marched behind the Offaly Banner, up Fifth Avenue, in the St. Patrick's Day Parade.

On the Gaelic Sport scene, all Offaly people were thrilled by the great victory achieved by the county hurlers in winning the 1985 All Ireland championship. We are happy to welcome the Offaly Captain Pat Fleury to our midst tonight and are honored to have the Liam McCarthy Cup present. Our own hurlers and footballers fought many a gallant fight in Gaelic Park this year and through championships have eluded us once again, all these players proved that Offaly truly earned the sobriquet "The Faithful County". They will surely be heard from in the not too distant future.

Tonight we will present the Patrick J. Grimes Memorial Scholarship Award for the seventh time and the Bill Fox Memorial Sports Award for the fifth time. It is fitting that we memorialize these two great Gaels every year in this fashion and also recognize excellence in our young people.

The Offaly Association will continue to grow only with the support of all and we urge everyone to join and become active in all our endeavors. It is our desire to have an Association that we can all be proud of and which truly represents the desires and aspirations of all our people.

A most enjoyable evening to all!

THE COMMITTEE

County Offaly Association of New York, Inc. 137

Guest of Honor

Denis McNamara

The County Offaly Association takes great pleasure in honoring tonight one of its most distinguished and generous sons. One word that would epitomize this Ballinabrackey native is "giving".Denis McNamara has given his all as a footballer and as a friend to so many that have come to New York seeking a helping hand. He has been a loving husband and father, a loyal supporter of Offaly and a benefactor of those in need.

Denis was born in Clonmore, Ballinabrackey to a farming family. His father, Roger is still hale and hearty at age 85 and living on the family farm. He cycles into Edenderry every day. Denis' late Mother, the former Elizabeth McNeil a native of Castlejordan, Co. Westmeath passed away in 1968. He is one of four sons and seven daughters.

A love for gaelic football developed early with Denis. As with most of the youth in north Offaly, the Gaelic Athletic Association

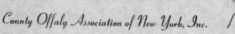

was the important social and athletic outlet for Denis McNamara. The first team that he played with was an old team called Clonmore Harps. He played with them in the Offaly junior championship for five years. A noted player with this team was Christy Darby, the father of the famous football family from Rhode (including tonight's Chairman, Sean). After Clonmore Harps disbanded, Denis played with Rhode for two years. At this point Father Callary organized the Ballinabrackey team and Denis was asked to play for his home Parish. Due to a strange ruling of the Leinster Council, Ballinabrackey was forced to compete in the Meath Championship, depriving Offaly of the services of Denis and the other great Ballinabrackey players for several years. Many of these great players gave distinguished service to Meath and were household names in football. In addition to Denis there was Kevin McNamee (who later played here in New York for Offaly), Peter Moore, Neddy Weir, Joe Carroll, and Christy Donoghue. Denis was selected on the Meath Team in 1951 and came to New York with the Meath team to play in the National League final against New York. Denis is a proud holder of a League medal as the men from the Royal county with their prominent Offaly contingent triumphed over the exiles, after besting Mayo in the home final.

Denis' first impressions of New York were not great and he returned home thinking he would never return. He later won a Leinster Championship medal with Meath. He played both midfield and right halfback.

Around that time Denis met his future wife, Mona Coyne in Edenderry. Mona encouraged Denis to go back to New York to start a new career. Denis communicated with Paddy Egan, the founder of Offaly football in New York and the late P. J. Grimes. Both of these men laid the ground work and Denis arrived in New York. Mona followed at a later date. He immediately started playing for Offaly football in New York. Denis played for Offaly for five more years before a broken leg cut short his playing career. But his love for football and hurling has never waned and he has continued to support the Games of the Gael. He has been a great financial supporter of every function that has been held over the years. He and Mona are in attendance at all things Offaly and many other Irish patriotic and charitable affairs.

After his arrival in New York, Denis entered the marble trade as a helper. After spending four months without finding employment, his perserverance paid off and he started in the trade that he has been associated with ever since. After 17 years working for various companies Denis decided to go into business for himself. He met a co-worker named Howard Fichtel who was also ambitious to improve himself and so Anolith Marble Co. was born. This company has done some of the most beautiful marble work in the City of New York. The Metropolitan Museum of Art, the Republic National Bank, the New York Stock Exchange, the American

(4)   132

County Offaly Association of New York, Inc.

Stock Exchange and the New Marriott Hotel at 46th Street and Broadway are just some of the projects that Anolith Marble has made a major contribution to. And needless to say, most of the employees of this firm are Irish and from the Faithful County. Denis has always looked after his own and never forgets the harsh times that he had to endure when he first arrived in New York. He has done so much to smooth the path for our young people and has provided employment for hundreds. He has never turned his back on anyone in need and continues to be of assistance to many.

As an athlete and a businessman, Denis McNamara has been very successful. But he is also a success in a much more important area. As a husband and father he is surrounded by a devoted and loving family group. His wife of 26 years, the former Mona Coyne, a native of County Meath seems to be still as taken with him as she was when they first met. In her own words, Mona said, "Denis is an excellent father and an excellent husband. I must say that down through the years he has definitely spoiled me. He never deprived me or the children of anything. His first concern has always been the welfare of the children and their education. He is very happy with them and very proud of them. We have had a wonderful 26 years together and I hope we will have many more years."

Daughter Caroline, a registered nurse and now the wife of Edenderry native Martin Murphy, recalls with great affection the deep concern that Denis has always showed for her welfare. Caroline said, "During all my time at school, Dad was always involved in my education. He always wanted to know what he could do to help me. He would never see me want for anything. He was a strict Father when I was growing up but he has always been generous, kind and never boastful. My husband and I both love him very much for all he has done for us."

Presently, Denis and Mona's son Roger is persuing his education in Dublin. He recently recalled the happy times he has had with his father. Roger said of his father, "he is the most decent guy in the world. He would do anything for you. He has done everything for me. He is kind and generous to all of us. And I know he loves me very much".

Tonight we gather with the family and friends of Denis McNamara to pay honor to him for all he has done throughout his years here in New York. We salute him as a footballer, an official, a friend in need, a devoted husband and a loving father. He is truly a son of the Faithful County. He has always exemplified the strength of character that is the pride of the people of Offaly. We all wish Denis and Mona the very best of health, happiness, peace and prosperity for many years to come. Every good wish is also extended to all the members of their families around the world who are with us in spirit, tonight.

113

The Edenderry gang is looking good as usual, wolfing with the hunger. There was P.J McEvoy, Jimmy Mangan, Pat Larkin, The Seery Brothers, Niall Dempsey, John Quinlan, Martin Murphy, Brendan Bergin, Paddy McCormack (The Iron Man) and the Darbys. This was all tied into the Hundredth Anniversary of the Offaly Association, of New York, This was like a going away party, and it turned out to be really great and they all enjoyed the American Football game, played at the Meadowlands New Jersey. The catering and the delicious food, the drink, all went down big time. I had a great chat with a lot of the prominent Offaly footballers, including Jody Gunning. I knew all the Gunning family. They were nice people. Nothing was ever held without the Casey's, Mick and Paddy; they were among my closest friends. Mona and I used to visit the Casey's in Rockland County for years. The girls are all married as they would say in Ireland; they all got good matches, all very nice guys. They are all doing well for themselves, couldn't happen to nicer people. They were the good old days. The Offaly contingent will be heading back after the weekend, most of them had relatives here, so it was an enjoyable reunion for all of them, and I am sure will be discussed for many a year. For me personally, it will be back to the grind stone. I don't know which direction to go...... Yes, it will be Boston.

I'll take the shuttle from La Guardia to Logan, thirty minutes. By car its three and three quarter hours. You have heard of Logan Airport and the infamous terrorists that flew out of Logan and knocked down the Twin Towers in lower Manhattan and killed more than three thousand innocent people,   it's not for me to comment on that fateful day, its part of history now.

From Logan to The Meridian is fast, five minutes by taxi. I talked to the foreman and Benny the draughtsman, everything is going along fine. No major problems. Seven foot space from floor to ceiling is the best we can do. A pity we can't sink the basketball players, one inch. If we could we'd be in business. But is hasn't become an issue, at least not yet. The workers are happy enough, they get paid every week, and Bill Bourke hasn't thrown me out of the Bank of Ireland yet. The lads are happy but said they could use a little more out of town money. We'll chat about that I said. After talking to my partner on the phone, we agreed to give them an extra thirty five dollars a week expenses. They were very thankful, and said they didn't want to be cutting into the wife's money. I must say that was very considerate of them. I'm not going to hang around here, now that diplomatic relations have improved with the workers, I'll head back to Riverdale, and see what Mona's up to. She has her own business to take care of, in Kittay House. She does well there. I told you about it earlier in the story. We have landed a new job, the name of the building, Carnegie Tower. We will be doing the whole lobby, a big job, all green marble, all from Italy. Very intricate, an artistic design. This gentleman, who will take complete responsibility for measurements and templates, and ordering from Italy requests that he not be named. He likes to remain anonymous. That is not a problem. Believe me that is a big responsibility, especially when you realize the material comes to about half a million dollars. Do you realize the load it takes off our shoulders? This will be worth seeing when it's installed; you could say really a masterpiece. My first job in the marble business was working for this gentleman, who at this time is working for us. The reason I call him a gentleman, is because he treated me like a real gentleman. What goes around comes around. Now I will treat him likewise, just like he deserves. I will just add, thanks Bob. That marble will be on the site in approximately three months.

Let me tell you about a great friend of mine, Mona and I were in touch with his wife Ann, by telephone. I should have said his grieving wife Ann, Leo O'Dowd, a great guy. Ann came on the phone crying. I instantly knew something sad had happened.

She said poor Leo, has Cancer of the Lungs, and he is dying, and I told Ann, that I was in a state of shock, and so was Mona. "I'll call you again in a couple of days". Mona and I said prayers for him and Ann. They are the most united couple I ever knew, and very popular and well known in both New York and Galway. Barna, in Connemara. I'll leave that sad story for now, and return later with hopefully better news.

We are now doing three fairly big jobs and also a few much smaller ones, and after those are all finished, I have a feeling we might call it a day, but thats down the road about two years. Meanwhile Mona and I will enjoy life and do our thing, like we always did. Spend a few months in Ireland about seven or eight, and the rest in Florida. The weather in Florida has to be seen to be believed. I met an elderly man on the beach one day and he stopped me and asked, if I ever heard of Paradise, and of course I said I did. "Well", he replied, "this is it, you're in it right here, in Palm Beach Florida." "I agree with you Sir, whole heartedly, and I am talking about the winter months". The summer in Florida averages about ninety five degrees Fahrenheit, that's why the snow geese return to where they come from, and only the natives are left, a mass exodus, from about the first of May until about the first of November. My son, his wife and the two boys live here all year around. He claims that you get used to it, and that you do whatever it takes to stay cool. Everything and every building, the cars, the supermarkets, are all air-conditioned; it's all a matter of getting used to the system. Mona and I love to come home to Ireland. We wouldn't miss the Racing Scene. We live fairly central to the Curragh, Naas, Fairyhouse, Punchestown and of course Kilbeggan, a great Farmer's meeting, and a chat with all the old friends, Martin Lowry, Tommy and Marie Scanlon, Declia Leech and Rita Kilduff, and Dan Walsh, poor Jack and Rita, have left the building R.I.P. Racing is not as well attended as it was during the Celtic Tiger. It has taken a beating in the U.S.A as well. The sign of the times, all over the world. Thank God, the terrorist that caused all this is gone. If there is a heaven and we Catholics believe there is, I don't think you'll be seeing him there. Thank the good Lord for his departure. As we bow our heads and humbly ask the good Lord, to rid the world of all real terrorists, and may peace spread across the nations of the earth and inspire its leaders to a lasting peace, Lord Jesus, Hear our Prayer. I'm not compiling a bible or anything of that nature, just passing on a couple of sincere wishes to my readers.

Mona and I are here now in Ireland and we fully intend to have a nice time. The nearest to us of course is Caroline our daughter, and Martin the Husband, the three children, Lauren, Evan and Karl. They usually join us when we go to the Curragh and after the races to the Hanged Man's restaurant. Mona's sister was with us in Florida, and flew home with us from Fort Lauderdale via New York, and after a couple of hours wait in New York, made comfortable in the V.I.P lounge, delicious food washed down with a bottle of Don Perignon, we boarded the plane in the best of spirits. You only pass this way once, do it with all the gusto you can muster up. Some people are afraid to let themselves go. It's hard to stay in the straight and narrow all the time. We have just touched down in good old Dublin; it's always nice to be home, no matter how often you do it. Caroline or Martin will be there to meet us no doubt. Through the customs and out the door and already on our way to Edenderry, Co. Offaly. We call it the Midlands. The routine breakfast at Caroline's. The kids are at school, and we will be up to Killane to unpack, and the usual couple of hours in the sack. The jet lag, strangely is much more tiring coming from New York to Ireland, than vice versa. Caroline and Martin always have a hearty little breakfast, we are more tired than hungry, but Ca insists on having the brecks. Snuggling in now, will talk to you all when I get up. I come out of this coma, back to the land of the living; we will freshen up with a shower, and be ready for the road again. Stacia and Pat invited us over for a quick visit. We dropped into see Angela and Jim on the way to Stacia's. They are well settled in and feel good. Over to Stacia's, they already know what to give us to drink, they have a lot of practice over the years. It will serve as an appetizer as we are on our way to Caroline's for dinner, also a strict routine over the years. We are now seated in Chestnut Lodge, having our dinner. It's as usual delicious. Mona and I will be doing a bit of travelling. We love to take a trip to Galway on the train. It's a great way to see the Irish Countryside as you speed along, you can see all the animals and some lovely country towns and villages. Hills, mountains and lovely fast flowing rivers and being the autumn, the golden barley fields, as well as wheat and oats, and the combines actually in the act of harvesting. It's actually entertaining as well as beautiful. Galway City itself is one of the best laid out and beautiful cities in Ireland. We head straight to either the Park Hotel, or to Leo and Ann's house in Barna, our very good friends over the years in New York. A beautiful five bedroom, four bath roomed house, overlooking the Atlantic Ocean. It's also beautifully landscaped, with little rivulets running under little bridges. You can hear it at night, the water trickling over the rocks and under those decorative little bridges. As Leo would say, "Not bad, for a Limerick Man", and Mona and I sitting back in lush ambience of a beautiful living room. And as our old Postman used to say," lowering a caution," his name Paddy Swords, from Tubberdaly outside the village of Rhode, County Offaly. That famous footballing village where many a famous county man played club football, with, just to mention a few and don't get mad, if I leave you out; The Casey brothers, Paddy and Mick, Paddy McCormack, Peter Leavy, the Kerrigans, The McNamees, The Quinns, Las Molloy, and many more that I can't recall right now.

Please forgive me, for leaving you out, after all I'm not a Rhode man, I did my best, what do want from a Ballinbrackey man. Most that I mentioned were good friends of mine, and some still are. My grandson Evan Murphy does weekends in O'Tooles bar tending. I knew the original owners. Pat Mulvin and his wife, we called her Ma Mulvin. Pat Larkin and I were often invited out by Pat Mulvin for a drink, privately in his living room. He knew he had the big C. then and would get very emotional. Understandably, may he rest in peace.

Now to something lighter. We are headed to the Curragh, with the grand children, at least some of them. Today it's just Lauren, and her mam Caroline. Mona and I, and I forgot Karl as well. We have mixed luck at the races, so we didn't do much damage. Racing over, we're now in the Hanged Man's restaurant knocking back a few and charring the owner Pat, a grand man. He runs a very good restaurant, and has an excellent clientele. You would never get a bad meal in the Hanged Mans restaurant. The Murphy family is off to Spain for a couple of weeks. Spain is nice and convenient for the Irish, and I believe the prices there are reasonable and the weather O.K also. A lot of Edenderry people go to Spain on holidays. What really makes it attractive is the reasonably short trip. The McNamara's from Florida are off to a few European countries, and will finish their vacation in Ireland for about ten days. I'm trying to arrange a golf game in Edenderry Golf Club, I am looking for a couple of left handed sets, as Roger's boys are left hander's, and a couple of golf buggies. I am looking forward to a game with them. Really hope the weather is good, that really makes it a lot of fun. I am constantly in touch with the jobs.

The Meridian and Boston, Newark, New Jersey, it's all going nicely and pretty much on schedule. But they all usually go past the estimated time. I'm banking heavy on Benny the draughtsman in Boston. He's a sharp dude. Big John is holding the helm in Newark, New Jersey and at Carnegie Towers. The material, marble, has just arrived on the job in Manhattan. I have a couple of old timers going to run that job. They have been around and know the business inside out. The man that measured and ordered the whole job, will go to the job site, and go through everything with the foreman. That is fantastic, he's a great guy, and we owe him a great debt of gratitude. He is an out and out professional, and has a huge talent. You are the greatest Bob. To be quite truthful we couldn't have taken this job only we knew he would take it on. I'll head back for the start, we will all meet, and get the show on the road, and of course, while I'm there, I'll drop over to Big John for a chat. I'll also be visiting the money source. The one and only Bill Bourke, at the Bank of Ireland, 5th Avenue, New York, that saint keeps all the wheels turning. I had a nice couple of weeks in New York and was happy with the way everything went. So now I feel more relaxed with all that behind me. It's a great feeling to know all is well and now of course it remains to be seen if it will all end well. We don't want any more like the one in New Jersey, again one hundred and fifty thousand dollars, we never got. At least I didn't get any of that; I do have suspicions about that one. Back again to the Old Sod.

Racing season is on. We are here most years for the flat racing season. We went to the Kentucky Darby; Aiden O'Brien had a horse running in it. We have a few bucks each way on him. We didn't fancy him; it was because he was from Ireland. He was drawn on the inside, which is the place to be if you have the speed to get away. Daddy Long Legs got away alright, and was in front briefly, but didn't stay there too long. After a couple of furlongs he was done and eventually finished last. I expect the jockey eased him back. No point in pursuing, he was never going to be placed. It was a very hot day and that would not be in his favor. Back to the Curragh next week and of course the Hanged

Mans'. Near the end of this true story, I will be writing a little more about my younger days in Ireland, as I didn't tell all that I should have, to be quite honest, it just came back to me later.

Right now we are in the Curragh and meeting some friends, that we enjoy and know for years, Michael and Therese, comes to mind quickly also Dessie from Galway and his wife, and of course Delia Leech. The Curragh couldn't function without Delia. We used to meet Benny and Sheila. Poor Benny passed away, that's Benny Powell for those who might not know him that well. We really enjoyed the chats with Benny and Sheila. He was very knowledgeable about all facets of the game, especially breeding, as was also his brother Leo. The crowds are not what they used to be. I could offer one reason, and that is, the admission fees are too high. It's that simple. The small crowds you see are mostly the same people all the time, the ones that can afford it. There are lots of people out there who would like to go racing, if they could afford the entrance fee. Families of three or four people will stay away. The racing authorities are shooting themselves in the foot, in my opinion.

I can go racing in the States for one third or less. Something is not right, but of course, I'm not running the show, just expressing an opinion for what it's worth. One of the most enjoyable racing days I have ever had was at Belmont Park, in Long Island, New York. One and a half miles on the dirt track, a stayers race no doubt, a beautiful Sunday afternoon. Mona and I, and four friends that we invited. On the way to the track I happened to spot, the world's best trainer, the man himself, the one and only Dermot Weld. I had met Dermot before a few times at the Curragh, so he knew me. I chatted for a few minutes with him and he talked about the horse he had running in the race, his name I'm sure will be familiar with racing fans. The horse's name was Go and Go. I remembered he told me he was a bit of a head case, temperamental. Let me tell all of you, there was no better man in racing to deal with a race horse of that nature, he gave him kid glove treatment, and understood a lot of his idiosyncrasies and that really helped with this particular animal. He got a good trip over and settled down nicely in his quarters at Belmont. So to make a long story short, I think he has a big chance, Dermot told me. Good luck Denis we will see what happens. Well of course what happened is history. Go and Go won by six lengths. By the way Mick Kinnane gave him a copy book ride, followed instructions to a perfection. Had him in all the right places at the right time especially at the finish line. One of the announcers wondered why Dermot Weld did not get an American Jockey to ride Go and Go, obviously he had not done his homework on Mick Kinnane. I think everybody except that announcer knows that Mick was a world class jockey. That glorious afternoon I will always remember, Mona and I and our friends, and what made it all the more enjoyable, we made a nice little killing at the tote, thanks to Dermot, and also Stan Cosgrove, the bossman of Moyglare Stud, who bred many a good one down the years.

I think the reason we, had so much interest in racing was because of the fact that my uncles were jockeys. Steeple chasing, Johnny McNeill and Tommy McNeill. Tommy rode in England, and Johnny in Ireland. Tommy was a bit more successful. He rode quite a lot of winners. The one horse in particular that comes to mind was a horse called "Airegead Sios". He won on him over thirty times, a two mile specialist. He rode him in the Aintree Grand National and he was a fence in front after two and a half miles. When he crashed out at the chair fence, the only way he would stay, the four miles, would be in a horse box. Tommy's relative and mine, is now training in England and let me tell you relatively successful. He has trained a good few winners, every year since he took up training about ten years ago. His son is showing promise and, at the young age of seventeen has ridden some nice winners. His grand-dad was Benny Powell, recently Swordestown Stud, and was very well known in racing circles, and also very popular and knowledgeable about racing and breeding. His brother Leo, Ex Goffs, and now "The Irish Field" (the boss man) is a regular encyclopedia of all facets of racing and the bloodstock industry. So now you can see I have, something in common with those Powells, I'm their first cousin. I meet John Weld now and again at the Curragh. He is married to Michelle Powell, Benny's daughter. John is a cousin of Dermots, and is a veterinary surgeon, got a lot of experience in the United States, and is a very keen follower of the bloodstock industry and racing.

Getting away from the sport of kings, and back to my own business, in the states, and all the time, planning the winding down of my own business, in the not too distant future. A couple of years perhaps, all going according to plan, as I said before. This is the Meridian Hotel in Boston, The Newark Rail Road Station, and Carnegie Towers. The three of them are fairly big jobs. They are all under way at the moment, and I brought little Benny, the draughtsman, back down to Carnegie Tower. It's complicated and he knows all the finer points of the marble business, and is needed by the men there. They have much more confidence, when he is at the job site. This is the Jewel in the Crown of the jobs we're doing. I'm out in Newark today visiting Big John, everything is going good there, fairly simple, as all the escalator bays, are identical. So when the first one was approved, it's repetitive all the way to the last one. Big John knows it's making a profit, so he will probably nurse it a bit. Remember its time, plus cost, I mentioned before in the story. Every sub-contractor would like a job like this one. All the lads we have want to go to Boston. Remember its room and board, and they usually make a few dollars on their expense money, that is after paying for the room and eating. Plus they have their wages sent home to the little women. That is the reason they were all hoping to be brought up to Boston. But on account of having to hire a percentage of locals, which was only fair, and that meant we were only able to take seven or eight, we did that, based on how long they were working for us, and that was also the fairest way to settle this situation. Meantime, the job is progressing satisfactorily, and we have a good idea when it will be completed. Meanwhile, when they remain in Boston, all is quiet in the home front. Roger has a job in Ireland, but his long term plans, means he will be bound for Florida, both him and his wife Majella, will have jobs to go to. Not too many Irish wind up in Florida. The summers there are quite hot, takes a bit of getting used to. Mona is going nicely in her own business. She has a captive audience. Her clients all live in the complex she works at. They are mostly wealthy Jewish people, and they actually love her. They made her a present of a beautiful gold chain for her neck, with a lovely charm on it, with her name is Yiddish. She loves working there, and it's just ten minutes from where we live in Riverdale.

It's that time of the year again; Mona and I are taking a trip to Ireland to visit our son Roger, and his wife Majella, and also of course, Martin and Caroline. We will enjoy being with them for the Christmas season. We hope to meet all or at least some of our friends and relatives. We will have a nice time, please God.

Yes, its two weeks later, and we have a lovely time, with most of the family and friends, and we got a lovely surprise with Larry and Eileen coming for a quick visit from London. They have a huge flat in the centre of London. It's nice to mix and have fun with those millionaire types. Great wine connoisseurs and we tasted quite a few bottles of it while they were here, and we like it also. Of course, the reason some of us like it was because the price was right, but all good wine, and good times come to an end and next week, as Mona would say, we'll be on chopped straws and buttermilk, and we will be back, once again to face the music. I will be headed for Boston and Mona to her place of business at Kittay House, where her beauty salon is located. Once we're back in the swing of things, we will be fine. But for now, we will rest up back in Riverdale, and resting up to freshen up for next week. It's a grand feeling to be well rested, and in the meantime, we will catch up with a few neighbors and friends, and exchange news, of what we all done around the holidays.

The next point of my story will surprise and astonish the younger generation. It's about the way the young people were brow-beaten in the years after we got our independence, and I'm sure before that as well, this pertains more to Rural Ireland and the farming community. The parents had one ambition only, and it was all about their daughters. Unless you were a farmer with a nice bit of land, you were at nothing and the older the better, it was a terrible attitude, and in reality, was like Penal Servitude, for their young and very often their beautiful young daughters, who had no say in the matter. Now having said that, I am going to give you two examples that are the Gods truth.

The first one is about a deal for a daughter, and that deal was consummated at a fair, a cattle fair, in Edenderry, Co. Offaly. I heard with my own two ears. I won't use the real names to protect the families that are still living. It went something like this; Mr.A to Mr.B said "you have a nice little girl out there in the street; I'd like to take her to be my wife". Mr.B said, "We can talk". To make a long story short, they settled the deal for this lovely young girl, with the following amount of payment, One Hundred Pounds, plus Two Bullocks that were right there on the street and Three Sheep from the farm at home. "When can I come and get her?", and the girl's father replied, "Give her a week to get her clothes together and be prepared". P.S, he was forty eight years old. Get this, she was sixteen. I had heard people talking about that kind of match making, but now I see the whole scenario and heard the whole deal. I mean, I have been at fairs before and saw cattle, pigs and sheep being sold, but this was a sickening first for me. This young lady had fifteen children for this man. I was personally more distressed than if this lovely young girl was laid to rest. That is one true story of mine; I have one more; this one is about another beautiful girl in her early twenties. The parents had the exact same ideas as that other catastrophe I am after telling about. This girl was a little bit older, about twenty one years old. Let me tell it this way. This girl had a nice young man in her radar. She met him about twice in the two years she had known him. The reason, she didn't meet him more often were two fold; one there was practically no transportation from where she lived in the middle of nowhere, and even if there were, the parents would not let her out of their sight. She could not understand why her sweetheart, gave up writing to her. You see when the mail man came to the door, and that wouldn't be often anyway, the parents would get the mail. She never suspected that they would keep the mail and burn it. What I'm saying is, he tried to get in touch with her, but the parents continually burned the letters. Let me tell you, the parents at the time had an old farmer just across the fields in mind for their beautiful daughter; only this one was seventy years old. How sad and how sick can people be? In my other true story, there was a thirty two year age difference, but in this one there is a forty eight year difference. Now if he was a Hollywood type and very rich, there wouldn't be a word about it, but this guy was an ugly old man, with no teeth, and probably never heard of deodorant, and if he did, would be too cheap to buy it. The parents forced her into marrying him. P.S, she had four children for him, and about four nervous breakdowns. If you could automatically bestow sainthood on a person, she would in my opinion be number one on the list. He passed away long before she was sixty. People thought when he passed away, that she would pick herself up and go out with her friends, but no she didn't. Her ego had long since disappeared. She was a broken woman, even her beauty had faded. She led a secluded life, even her childhood friends failed to motivate her, and she literarily faded into oblivion, with her only outing to mass on Sunday. Can you imagine a sadder story, I can't.

All over Ireland in those times, you could multiply these two stories by one hundred thousand times. In those times we were emerging from the Dark Shadows and Domination, that left its scars and inferiority complexes on us, but we have emerged, to be a modern society and can hold our own, with other nations and leaders of all countries. We have come a long way from the down trodden people of recent history. Whenever I talk to Americans about Ireland, those of them that haven't been to Ireland always express the wish that they would love to visit Ireland. Their friends told them of how friendly the Irish people were, they treat you like they would a member of the family. They have heard it from lots of people, who visited Ireland, how beautiful it is.

Right now, I am expecting a good friend of ours from Australia, Fr.Dan Moore. He calls to see us on the way to Killowen, and incidentally his first stop on his way home. A couple of appetizers (liquid) and maybe a bite to eat, and a lot of chatting, a year's worth, we have to make up. We will plan a little golf, and maybe a nineteenth hole chat over a Guinness. We always play a better game there than on the course. Liam Flynn, looks after us well at Edenderry Golf Course, it is one of the best, and almost always in great condition. I am planning a game about the first week in July. Roger, his two boys, Karl Murphy and I, and we are looking forward to that, maybe Martin will join us. We will see what happens. Mona and I have a bit of racing, the Curragh on Saturday, no doubt God willing we will be there, our first this year and more than likely, and The Hanged Mans' afterwards. We enjoy the food, and beverages, and a chat with Pat. It's only a skip and a jump from Edenderry, a half hour at the most. Caroline will be the chauffeur, she will bring some of her children, I'm pretty sure. This way she can have a beverage and enjoy herself.

Well we enjoyed the races yesterday and the meal last night. It was good to be out with some of the family. The kids like the races and have a couple of euro's each way and if they win a few bob, they are over the moon. We will stay another few weeks. We usually go somewhere with Martin and Caroline. Last year we really enjoyed the trip down south, and took in Moneygall on the way, and also the ferry from Kenmare, over to Clare and across to Doolin, an experience that is truly unique. A typical holiday resort with a difference. Those people are the heart and soul of Ireland, warm hearted and friendly. We visited Hayes Pub in Moneygall on the return. It's been standing room only ever since President Obama went into it, and drank a pint of Guinness. Would you believe I drank a pint from the same glass? His DNA had been carefully removed. They didn't want to mix him and I up. Ever since the President visited that town business has picked up at least three hundred percent. It's still absolutely amazing to see the crowds along the streets, tourists no doubt.

We went further south into Cork and stayed overnight in a nice hotel, food super – Dunraven Arms. We stayed downstairs after the meal and were feeling no pain, but really enjoyed it a lot. Where we are headed this year, I don't know yet.

I remember we were nine or ten months in the States, we had no car yet. Really where we lived, we didn't need a car. To be realistic a car would be a nuisance, you could spend an hour looking for a parking spot, and anyway public transport was the best. Express bus into Manhattan, outside our door. The Subway five minutes' walk, it went to all five boroughs. You really couldn't ask for anything better. They are the reasons we didn't have a car. Anyway this long weekend came along, and we, Mona and I decided we would rent a car for the long weekend.

We go to the car hire place, made the deal, three hundred dollars for the weekend. I handed the man the three hundred in cash. He said," Sorry sir, we don't take cash". I could hardly believe it. So he explained, "You see, with a credit Card, I have everything I want to know about you, with the cash, you could drive to Canada for instance, and never come back, and I would be out of a car. The credit card is our protection, against our cars been stolen". Yes, I understood. It's just common logic. Today everybody has a credit card, unfortunately as well as being used, they are also abused. People spend more than they can afford. They go bankrupt, and then the interest rate goes up and we all pay more interest. We have a system for years now. We use one Credit card, when the monthly bill arrives, we pay in full. You save yourself a lot of money. The interest rates would keep coming down, not up, if people paid their bills promptly. Then we would all benefit from it. A lot of people try to beat the system, and that's a fact. Bottom line, we did not have a car for the weekend.

I'm just glancing back over the years. Since I came to the United States, a lot of friends I knew in Ireland have gone to their eternal rest. Time keeps marching on, and a whole new generation has arrived on the scene, young and ambitious. We (us older guys) often say, "Amazing those young people, some of which will be running the country, and we wonder how you could find enough of them in this care free world, to do so". But history has taught us, that there will always be enough well educated and responsible young people, to take over the helm, when the older ones retire and hand over the reins. Over the years a lot of friends we knew came to visit us, mostly from Edenderry area, and of course some came out to work for us, and I must say they were good workers and they did not expect anything in the way of special treatment just because they knew me. They did an honest day's work and were treated fairly. My brother-in-law put it this way; Denny Mack was the Trail Blazer to the United States, and was nice to everybody that was invited to his house and believe me, there were plenty of friends and relatives, and family, and they all had a good time and were treated royally. Thank You Larry for those nice comments. Since then Larry himself, has gotten around the Globe and done very well for him, and Eileen. More Luck Larry, you and your Coyne Aviation deserve its success, it's not a given, you have to take it. Even at a very young age, around thirteen or fourteen years old, he showed "smarts". He could weigh up situations, like one day there was a horse running in England, his name was "Penny on the Jack". He was quoted on the daily paper at 33-1. So I gave Larry a bet to put on for me. A half crown each way. Se he figured out how many 33-1 shots has anybody ever won on. You would be lucky if you backed one or two in a life time. So he reasoned to himself – I'll do the bookie on this bet and I'll have give bob for myself, and also he thought, I never had five shillings in my life so far. Five shillings in the pocket, and that was that. P.S, you'll never believe it; Penny on the Jack won at 33-1. The poor little devil must have nearly died with embarrassment. I don't believe I ever brought it up to him to this day.

We are back in the States after a nice summer break, and also back to work, I was in constant touch all the time, so I knew what to expect, mostly all satisfactory, and heading for the date as anticipated. The one we admire the most is the job at Carnegie Towers. Its looks beautiful, a lovely design, with a very highly polished green marble. A couple of months should do it. The Meridian in Boston is also coming down to the wire, about three or four months. Time, its marching on, and there are other things in life besides working, in fact I'm looking ahead to a nice life, Mona and I, when I retire, and it will be Florida. We were there on our honeymoon. The beaches, the weather, especially in the winter, it has no equal. Plus the fact that my son has moved there, will be great. The small jobs we have are almost finished, give them a few weeks. I'm on my way up to Boston and I plan to stay a week there, and check everything out, and see if we have all the marble and granite we need to complete the job, as we got an additional extra, the elaborate beautifully designed entrance. Nice to get an extra, it sometimes makes the difference between breaking even, and making a nice little profit. I'll be with Little Benny, the draughtsman, laying out that entrance. That's really my reason for being here. The job otherwise is coming along nicely and better still we are looking now at about six weeks, Hallelujah. Can't wait to get all the contracts finished. But it takes time and a lot of work and some patience. I'll be here all week with Little Benny. During lunch, we discuss The Entrance. He brings a miniature set of drawings with him. We get into a corner, and don't bother anybody. The waitresses don't bother us, so there is no rush.

It's Saturday, I'm off back down to New York, and Riverdale. Mona has been on her own 'I hope', and we will have a nice meal together in 'The Coach and Four' restaurant. Joe Corning is the proprietor and always gives his customers a nice night cap, a liberal glass of Cognac, and the beauty of it, is its two minutes from home. The food is top class as well. Mona tells Joe a few old jokes, not too clean; he enjoys the not too clean ones, a dirty old man. Had a good night's sleep, Mass this Sunday morning in our Lady of Angels Church. Caroline and Roger went to the school in that Parish, so it re-kindles a few memories. Plus we know some old friends, among them, our best friends, Joan and Paddy Casey. We plan dinner in a couple of week's time. You guessed right, Joe Corning's again; I'll be looking forward to that. I'm downtown in the morning to Carnegie Towers. Well I'm here now, and at first glance everything seems to be fine, but it was very unusual to see the architect there, so I said to him, "Is everything alright", and he replied, "No, not exactly". I thought to myself, this is all I need. So I said, "What might be the problem?" he replied quickly, "The green is not the right shade". So I said, "Is it not a bit late now that you noticed this problem", and he replied, "I'm going from memory, and misplaced the original sample". So I suggested that we meet again in the morning, and I would have the original sample. "O.K", he agreed. That episode puzzled me, so I kind of thought, this might be a story he manufactured, but I'll wait and see what tomorrow brings. I arrived the next morning with the sample, with an approved stamp on the back of it. The architects stamp of approval. Lo and Behold, he didn't show up. I said to the foreman, "Surge ahead, everything is now one hundred and one percent perfect". I had no doubt about that what so ever. The foreman told me he was running a job a few years ago, and the very same problem came up, and there was nothing wrong, just like here. So now you know and we all knew what the real problem was. He apologized after, by explaining, he was in Vegas, doing a spot of gambling, and lost a good bit of money. So he asked if I could help, that he would greatly appreciate it. I can't comment on that at this time, but I can tell you the job is getting close to finished, and it's really beautiful.

I'm playing a game of golf with Roger and his friend, The Juke. It's some kind of a tournament, and Roger, The Duke and I are playing in it. Those outings are great. They give you all kinds of goodies going out, even the golf balls. You should see the spread, at the nineteenth hole; you could eat a fourteen ounce steak and half a chicken, if you were able, and twenty four ounce mugs of beer, every brand of beer on draught. I've done it a few times with Roger, it's really something else. I'm going out to see Big John in New Jersey tomorrow, but I have to sleep off this food and beer from yesterday. The beer hangover is enough, not talking of the food, a double whammy. Martin Murphy would love that kind of an outing especially those twenty four once beers in a jug. Now I'm here, hangover gone, in New Jersey, visiting Big John, and he never had it so good and he told me so. But he added, "You Denis, never had it so good either". He is right, like I said before, this is the way to go, Cost Plus – the Plus in case you were wondering is the profit you get out of the job, what you are allowed, and in this case thirty three percent profit. They don't come too often like this one, and for Big John, he could almost walk to the job. We had lunch together, all Big John ate was six hamburgers and six sides of fries on the side. He said he's cutting down. He used to do twelve hamburgers and six sides of fries, it's true, because on one job Big John was on, my son Roger used to go for his lunch with him. Roger said on top of two sixteen ounce Pepsi colas, just fifteen minutes, everything would have disappeared. He only weighed three hundred and fifty pounds – in stones that come out to be twenty five stone. I wonder how he would do in a pony and trap years ago! It's well known the Roto Reuter knows exactly where he lived. But really there only one Big John, right now on this job. He is in his glory, everything going according to plan. Big John came to Ireland a few times, and he got along great with the people. He was hail fellow, well met, and he never shied away from the counter when it came to his time to buy. In fact the opposite, he often bought out of his turn, and would talk about his days as a professional base ball player. I believe he was a good player. I won't be seeing John for a couple of weeks now. Mona and I are heading down to Florida, for a week or so, Killian, Roger's oldest boy is getting confirmed. The one thing about Florida, it won't be cold anyway. I might get in a few holes of golf. You rarely see anybody walk on the golf course, it's a bit hot, so we drive the electric carts. Actually they don't let you walk on most of the courses, walking also slows up the game, and that's true. This is Saturday, and we are on our way down to St.Vincent Ferere, Catholic Church for

Killian's Confirmation. We are going to celebrate the occasion at the Ritz Carlton, near where we all live. Looking forward to that, just immediate family. Really none of us have relatives in the area! After the celebrations, we are off to Orlando. Roger has a nice spacious condominium there, three bedrooms, three bathrooms, and it happens to be overlooking the eighteenth green. We watch the golfers pass by from the terrace, and tomorrow, or the next day, we will play out there. We spent this evening at the miniature golf place. The kids love any kind of activity, of course, I mentioned before, their game is Ice Hockey. They play that every week, at least twice. Killian has his sights set to do something in the N.H.L, what it will be, he doesn't know at this time. But Mona and I say prayers, that he will do something good or maybe big in the hockey organization. Mona and I wish him well. We spent the week in Orlando. Roger, the boys and I played in their golf course, a couple of times. I call it their golf course, because their condo is actually part of that whole development. It's a big course, seven thousand, four hundred yards, much too long for me these days. The main thing is we had a lot of fun. Tarin is very competitive, so he and I have a kind of a private little tournament. It never has come to punches, not yet anyway, one thing we always look forward to is having a good shower, freshening up, maybe snooze for about forty five minutes, have a nice cocktail and head out to one of our favorite restaurants, one of them being Longhorns'. Delicious big juicy tender steaks, starters of your choice. We don't ever rush. We spend a couple of hours and enjoy the moment, and thank the good Lord for the ambience, and the great company I often say, we'll be a long time dead. However I don't completely agree with the cliché, Eat, Drink, and be Merry for tomorrow we Die. Speaking about tomorrow, we will be heading back to Palm Beach, and have a couple of days to spend there, Mona no doubt will be visiting some of her clients, but she will be seeing all of them later on in the year. We, Mona and I will take a quick visit to Brogue's Pub, in Lakeworth and then over to another friend of ours, Clem McCauley, who used to run Brogues, but is now here, in this magnificent pub, "Slainte", it's in Boynton Beach, a real up market spot with the result, they get quite a lot of up market clients, and that never hurts. If you are ever in the Boynton Beach area, call in to see Clem McAuley, you will be glad you did. We are having a bite to eat thee now, it looks good and it's as delicious as it looks. We are on our way back up to Palm Beach to meet some friends from Ireland that we are taking out to dinner. Home again, we will probably take a nap and be fresh for dinner. I'm sure you have heard of Tommy and Marie Scanlon. They have been in the Pub business for many years, around Kinnegad, Mullingar, and Edenderry. So we won't be short of chat, and we're sure to get all the pub and racing news. Tommy would have made a great commentator in racing. He has the ability to talk constantly; the only thing that stops him is when he is eating. Marie would chat if she got a chance, but we had a lovely dinner in one of our favorite spots, Longhorns'. The steaks are the best and we talked about old times. Mona of course, knew the Scanlon's long before I did, so she got in her licks, and when she gets going, she would remind you of old Larry Coyne. Loud and Clear, and you better not question her when she has the floor.

At the minute, we are waiting for Fr.Dan Moore to come home, as he does every year about July first. This is actually his fiftieth year as a priest and no doubt in the world, he will be celebrating his golden jubilee and also I heard that it will be open house, for the parish and surrounding parishes. Well anyway it will be a wonderful and memorable get together, and that is a lovely occasion to look forward to, and of course the celebrations will be held in the old homestead where there have been many, many celebrations. Many memories from the past celebrations and parties. I don't want to make anybody feel sad, especially the

Moore family that are still with us, but what I've said is an ideal introduction to quote a few lines from an old song, and it goes something like this; "Lonely the house now and lonely the moorland, the children are scattered, the old folks are gone. Why stand I here like a ghost in a shadow, its time I were moving, but not time yet to move on". I didn't continue with the words of the song because it would be inappropriate at this time in history not to carry on. The house is a lasting monument to all the Moore of the past, as it will be to all the Moore's of the present, and may the Lord have mercy on Neddie and Phyllis, they were part of the whole equation.

Back to work now, you can't party all the time; it wouldn't be good for your health or your bank balance. I'll be heading back to Boston. Before this job is finished I'll know my way around Boston fairly well. It's such a great city; the young people keep it buzzing and all the colleges, universities, and schools of all denominations. The city comes really alive in the summertime. The long evenings, the sidewalk cafes with not an empty seat, a great distraction to my young workers. Beautiful young ladies, dining in the sidewalk restaurants, and cafes, and the fact that's it very hot in the summer months, the young ladies are scantily clad and that even more attraction to my young lads. But that's O.K; it's a very normal reaction. Don't you think? Good, I'm glad you agree. I'll be on the job in the morning, and back to the serious business of getting this job finished. It hasn't too long to go now, about one month. Benny, the draughtsman, would like to get a break, and it won't be too long now. Three days have slipped by already and Benny and I have, pretty much gone over everything, and we will discuss it further now, sitting at the Diner, having a bite to eat. Benny has a list of all the odds and ends of the whole job and this will be my second last time here on this job all going well. That is our intension, as of now, but you have heard the old cliché, "Hell is paved with good intentions", but we will keep our fingers crossed and hope for the best. I know when the guys are not complaining about anything, they must be happy enough. I know when I worked for somebody else; I would speak to the foreman and explain my case. Dealing with problems and complaints is all part of doing business, they call it the norm. I'll go along with that. My week here in the nicest city on the planet, has come to and, I'll be on my way back again to Riverdale and home to visit the War Department, indeed it's a long long way from that, one thing about Mona, she always welcomes me home. When she stops doing that, I'm in trouble. Never happen, (hopefully). We will go out this evening to our local great restaurant, Joe Corning's. Have a nice meal, and couple of appetizers, a chat with our good friend Joe. We have been going to his place for years to see how they are doing. We are coming down to the wire with all the jobs, and to be honest I'm looking forward to it, I can't wait for the day, when I can say, I have completely done with all the jobs, because it's not easy and it's a lot of pressure. Thank God for the good health he gave me, without which, I couldn't have carried on, when I look back on all the jobs, and all the different guys we employed over twenty years, all different personalities, I nearly always made each on the them feel, as they were really the best worker I ever had, sometimes that works, but not all the time. The smart ones are in it for a decent weeks wages and don't care much whether you like them personally or not, and that makes sense. We had workers from different countries, mostly Ireland, but they all got along together, which is pretty amazing. All with one goal in mind, making a living for their families. The good old United States itself is the great melting pot for people from almost every country in the world, about two hundred different nationalities it is reckoned. Helping them and in doing so, helping to strengthen, the greatest economy the world has ever known. But even, the

United States is feeling this awful recession. Nobody escaped this one, but we have to tighten our belts and look forward to an improving economy. It will come when the last of the toxic debts are resolved. Hopefully soon so we can get back to a little prosperity once more. Right now I am looking forward to getting the last of the jobs finished, so I can retire down to a warmer climate, which will be Florida. Roger is already there and Majella as a matter of fact. They have bought a home there in a very nice area and Mona and I would like to get a condominium somewhere near them. The winters there are great and we are looking forward to living there for the winter months, but that is a little while down the road. But again, first things first. I am on a mission to get the jobs finished. Boston will be finished first, and I'm going there tomorrow. I'll stay a couple of days, three with Benny the draughtsman; we will estimate a finishing date. I'd say roughly three weeks from now. I'm here with Benny, and we have agreed on about three weeks. I've spent three days here so, its time to go back to Mona, Mona who keeps the home fires burning and is quite capable of doing so, and its great to be home, be it ever so humble, there is no place like home. The usual nice dinner, this time at home, no better woman to put one on the table. A couple of friends join us for dinner, Ann and Leo O'Dowd, a great chat, and some refreshments, we talk about old times. Leo and Ann just bought a lovely house in Barna, outside Galway City, and we told them we were planning to buy a house in Edenderry, Co. Offaly. So with God's help we will be able to find a house that we like in a nice part of town. Mona has a lot of family in the area, her sister's Stacia and Angela, Caroline our daughter and her husband Martin, and several cousins in the area. So we will be back really among relatives and friends and that of course if something else to look forward to, meanwhile at this time, I am trying to get finished up with the jobs. The first one will be Carnegie Towers, one more week, and that should do it, what sweet relief that will be, it was the most nerve racking, with such a delicate and artistic design. But thank, the good Lord and the marble setters, we are almost there. But Boston will be slightly in front, with Boston out of the way and finished. They are down to the Punch list there. We will be back to the local jobs, and there will be no more long distance travelling, that will be a big help. The finish there is within days, they don't need me up there until, I get the call for the last inspection, with Benny and the architect. I am out here now with Big John in New Jersey. "No problems out here", says Big John. I'm milking it the best I can, of course John knows we are about to retire, and he also knows it will be his swansong. I'm sure the Reader will get the picture. I never get much of a chance to go out to visit the shop in Queens and my partner Howie, but I'm on my way now. Haven't been there for two months. There is nothing ever too exiting there, except the humdrum and noise of the machines. The good thing about that is the workers can't hear each other talking, so they don't bother. They keep on grinding and polishing Howie, my partner is happy enough to stay in the office. He also keeps on eye on the lads in the shop, but that's more or less a matter of form as they are all good at their own particular jobs. He also keeps the requisitions for money promptly up to date. That is vitally important, when you are running a business. Now I'm on my way back to Boston, it's finally finished. Benny called me and told me so. We will make the last inspection with the architect. When I get there tomorrow we check everything, and when there is a clean sheet, the job is closed for final payment, signed and sealed. All the workers are invited to the finish of the job Party, Friday evening. I'm going back home now, for a couple of days, and will be back here in Boston, Mona of course will be on board and we are looking forward to a good night. I personally feel the pressure is off, and time for a bit of celebration with all the workers. If should be a great evening meeting all the workers, our own, and all the other trades, you get to know over the course of fourteen months. Its Tuesday, the party is Friday; I have a couple of days to visit Carnegie Towers, and New Jersey. Well Big John is as big as ever, happy as Larry but realizes he can't milk this job much longer, as much as he would like to. He might stretch it for another three or four week's top. "Do the best you can John, see you soon", I said. I'll go to Carnegie tomorrow, Mona and I are going out to our old favorite spot tonight, you guessed it, The Coach and Four. The one and only Joe Cornys. I'm tired, a little snooze and a shower, and I'm ready for a nice meal, and let me tell you, that all you ever get from Joe. Mona likes the food here also, I don't want to bore you with the details, so I'll just say, we both settled for Chateaux Briand. It's always the specialty of the house; people come from all over New York for it. Tonight was no different. Chatted some with Joe and his wife, who is the Maitre d', a sweet person, always a smile on her face, out usual complimentary Brandy Hennessy, on the house, smooth as silk. Time to leave here, which is always difficult. We are in the mood to sack out and have a good sleep, and tomorrow, dawn to Carnegie Tower where I will get together with the foreman and estimate when we will finish up here. We come to the conclusion, that two weeks should wind it up, and that's good to see the light at the end of the tunnel. Tomorrow night is the party in Boston; I heard Mona say, "what would be appropriate to wear". That's always a bit of a problem, to figure out, so I told her , "if this will help you, there is a band,, and a dance floor, So I suppose you could wear something dressy, you can figure out what that might be. That's the only help I can give," As any lady that knows Mona can tell you she is known to have a few different outfits. I have no doubt that she will pick the appropriate one. We are now on our way to the party, it's a nice bright evening. I decided to drive; it's about three and three quarter hours. That will get us to Boston at around seven o'clock, nice time; seven thirty is the starting time. We will mingle at the bar in the lounge, renew friendships, meet as many people as we can, mostly those that worked in the reconstruction of the hotel, probably have a cocktail, with a few close friends. Before we take our seats, I requested a large long table to hold our own New Yorkers, and the workers from Boston that we had for the duration of the job. A table for twenty six, Mona and I, and twelve each from New York and Boston, twenty six at our table. I had no problem with our request; we are all seated and ready for a lovely evening. I had a special seat at the end of the table. For our guest of honor, call that the head of the table - my partner Howie. The waiter came with bottles of our choice, Red and White, plenty of it, and whatever spirits we needed of our choice. The food menu was lavish, soup to nuts and everything else as well. After about an hour, when we are all stuffed with food and whatever, we are all in high gear and enjoying every moment of it, talking to my many acquaintances, from the job it was like the evening flew by. The band strikes up, very modern, and some old numbers, made for a memorable night, in this refurbished, old post office, into a modern, beautiful hotel, The Meridian. I am personally proud and with a sense of achievement, that we had an important park in making this old post office into a modern hotel, after all, the entrance lobby is your immediate and first impression, and that was a lovely design of Italian Bottisceni Marble, manufactured and finished in Italy. It will be there, as our display of how capable we are of producing a finished product that we know, will stand the test of time, and be a great example of what Anolith marble company can do. The sub contractors got a chance to say a few words, but keep your little speeches short, and they all complied. I got my say in also, and got the biggest ovation. Not because of the brilliance of my little speech, but because I spoke with a "brogue". We were all getting a bit tired, and the crowds were about to start saying their goodbyes and that took the best part of an hour. Mona was also tired but was delighted with all the lovely people she met, quite a few of them from Ireland.

So that's the end of a great experience. I take away with me many lasting memories, and also the very nice people I came in contact with as we draw down the curtain, on yet another job successfully completed, and head back home, to Riverdale.

Mona and I will take a break for a few days, probably in Palm Beach, Florida. A great place to relax. We know a good few people down there. The most, and best courses, golf that is, practically every golf course, except the exclusive ones, are accessible to the public. Green fee and electric cart, most courses don't allow you to walk because it slows up the game, it takes too long, with the golf buggies they can get more people on the course and that simply means more revenue. Makes sense really, plus the temperature is at least eighty degrees Fahrenheit. You also get a nice breeze on the carts, which is great. We will play "Rolling Hills", where we have a condo. We don't stay in the condo, it's rented out. We usually stay in a motel near where we are going to play. There is a great choice of restaurants everywhere in Florida, and we get together with some friends we know. We will be seeing Roger and family also. There is never a dull moment when we go there, on the move all the time.

We would give the children more time when we were in Ireland as you will see, they were not too long in school here in Ireland. We all miss each other very much, but I'm back now, and its three weeks later, trying to finish up the remaining few jobs. Tomorrow I'm out to New Jersey to pay off the men, and that will bring that one to a close. Yes, it's Friday, and I am on my way to Newark, New Jersey, with the pay and the pink slips, never too welcome with the men, but good for them, there is plenty of work at the moment, and we chatted over lunch together. That would be my last treat to them, sorry to let you go Big John. We had a good relationship, and life goes on, nobody is indispensable, life teaches us that. Goodbye Big John, keep in touch, and I'm sorry that one is over. That was a lovely money spinner, the best job in many ways we ever had. Tomorrow down to Manhattan to finish up the last two small jobs. They will be completed; I just spoke to Willie Lowry. He ran the two of them, the same Willie Lowry, was a great hurler and footballer with Westmeath. He will tell you himself, that he done fairly good with us, he made some serious money with us. The one in New Jersey was the best, him and Sean Darby done that one. Darby was from around Rhode, Co.Offaly.

So I am down here now with Willie, sorry of course it has to be a pink slip. But Darby and Willie will get a job in the morning. They know how to produce the goods on the job. We had a beer and I paid them, and we were on our way. They were dropping off the station wagon and all the tools at the shop in Long Island City, this evening.

That Ladies, and Gentlemen, is the end of the road for another marble corporation, twenty years may not seem too long, but I for one have had enough. It's a tough, dog eat dog business. I could add cut throat, but I'm not sorry or complaining. I went into it with my eyes wide open, I spent twenty years, working for marble companies, and I learned every trick in the bag about the installation of marble out in the buildings. I could set marble better than ninety per cent of the installers, so I wasn't getting into something I knew nothing about, far from it. The one big negative was competing against, the biggest companies in the businesses that were established, before I knew what a piece of marble looked like. But I knew what the price of labor was, and how much a team could produce, as good as or better than most. A team was two men, a helper and setter. In my experience, the helper that had experience was usually smarter than the setter; be that as it may, I could with no problem estimate the labor. I could get a brochure from the material suppliers, with all the difference prices, put the material price and the labor price together, and then what profit you wanted. The usual rule of thumb was; thirty-three and a third material, thirty-three and a third labor, and thirty-three and a third profit, subject to slight changes, depending on the location and difficulty of the job. So pricing was not our initial problem. The real problem would be to try and get a job, and bid against, the big established companies. How do you even go about that problem? You can be a professional at pricing, but if you can't get a job you're at nothing. Let me tell you this, during my twenty years working for other people in the marble business, I did get to know a good few Supers on jobs, did some of them personal favors, so they said, they owed me, and if, and when you get into your own business, keep in touch, which I always did, and right off the bat, and I can't mention the name of that company, he told me, "my company actually is overbooked with jobs, we will bid on the job, but will bid at least twenty percent higher than we normally would, hoping we don't get it and even if we do, I will go to bat for your company, just have a little patience and you will have your first job, a nice relatively straightforward, large areas with fairly big marble panels. I'll let you know as soon as I have all the information. Make sure Denis; don't bid that job up front".

O.K, I am keeping my fingers crossed, as this will be, if we get it, a history maker for our company. Right now I am going around in circles, trying to finish up little private deals, I had cooking. But just now, which is only three weeks, since I spoke to my friend, the Super', for that big company, he said, "we landed that big job and I have it set up with my boss, you submit a price, I will give you a ball park figure to go by. Check it yourself, on the blue print, that I will send you. We will do this all very quickly and you and your company will be on your way with your first job. How about that Denis? I knew let it go long or short, I was going to do you a favor". So I told him, how much I appreciated all that, and we will get together shortly. We got together when I took him and his friend and their two wives out together, for dinner, and we celebrated big time. Mona of course was with me, in our favorite restaurant, The Palisadian, in New Jersey, after all this was our first job. I can tell you now, it was a big simple job, and we made a handsome profit. I will always remember my friend, as I look back on it now. It put us right up there with the big guys and most of them didn't like a bit of it, but we loved it, and I can tell you now, twenty years later, we never looked back, and the world was not a bad place anymore. It goes to show you, never give up; you never know what's around the corner. That one job that a good friend secured for us could easily have been the difference between success and failure, is now history. It put us on the map, and except for a couple of jobs in those twenty years, we were very successful, and sticking with us all the way was a great friend, Manager of the Bank of Ireland, New York, Bill Burke, a Mayo man. He trusted us and we never let him down and we parted the way we started, the best of good friends. The man we bought the factory from, another great gentleman, I had often worked for him, down the years, and he was delighted to sell to me, and when we decided to sell, we will be doing very well, as already we have had a bid, and it's seven times the price we paid for it. Prices have sky-rocketed since we bought twenty years ago. That's not hard to take.

This name Dessie Keogh, a friend and his wife Christine, he is from Multyfarnham in County Westmeath, and Christine is American born. Christine is an interior decorator and designer. Christine actually suggested the title for my life story, and that name was simply, "Denny Mack". So I'm going with that name.

Dessie, is also in the marble and stone business. He does mostly cladding on the exterior of buildings. Heavy limestone and granite. We visit the Keogh family, and lunch together at least once every summer. We also get together with the Larkin's Pat and Stacia, Caroline, Martin and family, Marie and John Joe. This year we have had quite a bit of rain. It really doesn't make much difference except on the little jobs in the garden. You don't come to Ireland to get a tan. Mona and I like to go racing. The wet weather does take a toll on that sport, but we like the Curragh and Kilbeggan, as they are convenient, and we have a favorite restaurant, that is on the outskirts of the Curragh Racecourse. The name of the restaurant is "The Hanged Mans". The owner takes your dinner order, his name is Pat, and he tells good jokes and doesn't charge a penny for them. The food is delicious and that's the reason it's always packed with people. Another good friend just celebrated his golden jubilee as a priest, Fr.Dan Moore. Mona and I were at the celebrations, we had a lovely time, meeting a lot of old friends there, Kevin McNamee and his lovely wife Maureen and all the Moore family, that are still with us, and of course, at least half the parish of Ballinabrackey and Castlejordan. Unfortunately there are less and less golden jubilees, with all of the modern distractions there are, it's hard to blame the modern day priest for leaving the church, but it is the reality of today's modern world. In my young days, the ladies wore dresses about nine inches below their knees, but today it's exactly the opposite, nine inches above their knees. Let's face it we all look, and that includes, priests, ministers and rabbis, old and young. The ladies also wore long knickers with an elastic band at the bottom, just above their knees. It was black elastic, and printed in white letters were the words, "Thou shalt not pass". Let's face it, we are all human, all the rules and regulations were manmade, by the church. My personal opinion is that all those laws and rules of the church need a re-think. I know you could get a lot of support on that issue.

I had a few loose ends to complete and finish up, as my partner skipped away for good to Florida. That wasn't a nice thing to do, was it?. But you can't beat a true friend, and that true friend was Gerry O'Sullivan, "the Kerryman". He told me, "Denis make a list of what's to be done, and I'll take care of it". Isn't that a real friend? I made up the lists, and they were on three different jobs. Two weeks later he called me, and said "the jobs are completed". I also got a work release to send in a requisition for the remaining money, that we were owed. It made life so much easier for me, as I was now completely on my own, except for my one and only, Mona. We have a dinner planned. Mona and I, Gerry and his wife, and that will be the most enjoyable dinner we had in a long time, and of course to settle up with Gerry. I'm really over the moon about that. I have sent in the last of the requisitions. When I get paid, which should be soon, the real final chapter will be in place, to officially end the life of Anolith marble. It was a long ride and like life itself, had a few lows, but thank God, mostly highs. One rotten apple doesn't destroy all the apples, when it's detected in time, and dealt with immediately, and I made sure of that. The individual, who was stealing big, I heard he had all kinds of bad health and bad luck. I won't be mourning for him, I assure you. I met a lot of people, a mixed bag, mostly people that would do me a good turn. People I should not forget like Niall and Ann Dempsey, they would do you a good turn at a drop of a hat, and often did, with them, I am never stuck for golf clubs, left-handed or right-handed, like recently I had three visitors from the states, Roger my son, and his two sons, Killian and Tarin. Where would I get left-handed clubs at short notice, from the Dempsey's who else. I suppose that what friends are for.

We had one problem, we got wet to the Colons, but we got in the round. Thanks also to the Pro in Edenderry, Ken O'Brien, extremely helpful, and also Liam Flynn, the bartender. Everybody is so nice out there. Martin Murphy is a kind of boss-man out there. He carries a lot of clout. Martin is the only golfer I know that improved with age. I'd like to recognize the local clergy, the very Reverends' P.J McEvoy, John McDonald, and the curate Greg for all their prayers, and kind wishes, also in my old parish of Ballinabrackey, the Reverend Fr.Halpin, a lovely man, and of course our friend for a number of years, Fr.Dan Moore, originally from the Parish of Ballinabrackey and Castlejordan, but in Australia for the past fifty years, a big-time G.A.A man, as were all the Moores' for a hundred years at least. Say Hallo to Fr.Teddy Mullano, a true Kerryman. I am really coming to a close now, and thanks to my daughter Caroline for all the help over the years, and Martin and the three children, Lauren, Evan and Karl. To Roger, Majella, and the two boys, thanks.

To finish this story, is very hard. It's like rolling down a hill, in an empty barrel. So let me go out in style. Whatever I wrote in this story is as far as I know True. It is a true story of most of my life, and let me tell you this, the luckiest day of my life, was the day I didn't get the old farm at home in Clonmore. It was the day, my father said to me, when I asked him for the farm, he had a couple of drinks taken, he said, "You are pissing up stream without a paddle against the Wind". So, I just plainly said to him, "I'm bound for America". Not alone did he not give me any money; he didn't even wish me luck. Mona, god love her, Jane, Mick Moriarity and Ollie Powell, my cousin, left me down to Cobh. They stayed the night with me and the next morning we had breakfast together, and there was a sad couple of hours waiting to go on the ship. We parted a couple of tears later, I was on the ship waving. "So long, but not goodbye". Three months later, Paddy Egan, a great friend went to meet Mona at the airport, "Kennedy", and we really enjoyed our reunion. We were both very happy. I had a lovely room for Mona with a Galway lady, but later she moved closer to where I had an apartment, to another Galway lady. That made Mona happy. Two years later, we were married in St.Patrick's Cathedral, and the rest is history.

My story from the time I first went to school in Castlejordan.

I will say "So Long now", and hope that some people might have the patience to read my story. I'm not a professional story teller, but you might get something out of it, if I didn't bore you with all the details, but I had to do it that way because it was part of my story, and I told it, in my own way.

The truth is I didn't have help from anybody..... My sincerest good wishes to those that read it. My thanks to those who insisted that I write my story?

Thanks to all,
Denis McNamara